HUMPHREY BOGART

HUMPHREY BOGART

A Pyramid Illustrated History of the Movies

by
ALAN G. BARBOUR

General Editor: **TED SENNETT**

PYRAMID
PUBLICATIONS
NEW YORK

Dedicated to my stepfather
Howard G. Marriott
with deep affection and gratitude.

A Pyramid Illustrated History of the Movies

Copyright © 1973 by Pyramid Communications, Inc.

First edition published February, 1973
Fifth printing September 1975

ISBN 0-515-02930-0

Library of Congress Catalog Card Number: 72-93667

Printed in the United States of America

Published by Pyramid Publications, a division of Pyramid Communications, Inc. Its trademarks, consisting of the word "Pyramid" and the portrayal of a pyramid are registered in the United States Patent Office.

PYRAMID COMMUNICATIONS, INC.
919 Third Avenue, New York, N.Y. 10022

Pyramid Communications, Inc.

PYRAMID COMMUNICATIONS, INC.

PREFACE

By TED SENNETT

"The movies!" Flickering lights in the darkness that stirred our imaginations and haunted our dreams. All of us cherish memories of "going to the movies" to gasp at feats of derring-do, to roar with laughter at clownish antics, to weep at acts of noble sacrifice. For many filmgoers, the events on the screen were not only larger than life but also more mysterious, more fascinating, and—when times were bad—more rewarding. And if audiences could be blamed for preferring movies to life, they never seemed to notice, or care.

Of course the movies have always been more than a source of wish-fulfillment or a repository for nostalgic memories. From the first unsteady images to today's most experimental efforts, motion pictures have mirrored America's social history, and over the decades they have developed into an internationally esteemed art.

As social history, movies reflect our changing tastes, styles, and ideas. To our amusement, they show us how we looked and behaved: flappers with bobbed hair and bee-stung lips cavorting at "wild" parties; gangsters and G-men in striped suits and wide-brimmed hats exchanging gunfire in city streets; pompadoured "swing-shift" Susies and dashing servicemen, "working for Uncle Sam." To our chagrin, they show us the innocent (and sometimes not so innocent) lies we believed: that love triumphs over all adversity and even comes to broad-shouldered lady executives; that war is an heroic and virtually bloodless activity; that fame and success can be achieved indiscriminately by chorus girls, scientists, football players, and artists. To our edification, they show us how we felt about marriage in the twenties, crime in the thirties, war in the forties, big business in the fifties, and youth in the sixties. (Presumably future filmgoers will know how we felt about sex in the seventies.)

As an influential art, motion pictures are being studied and analyzed as never before by young filmgoers who are excited by the medium's past accomplishments and its even greater potential for the future. The rich body of films from *Intolerance* to *The Godfather;* the work of directors from Griffith to Kubrick; the uses of film for documenting events, ideas, and even emotions—these are the abundant materials from which film courses and film societies are being created across the country.

PYRAMID ILLUSTRATED HISTORY OF THE MOVIES also draws on these materials, encompassing in a series of publications all the people, the trends, and the concepts that have contributed to motion pictures as nostalgia, as social history, and as art. The books in the series range as widely as the camera-eye can take us, from the distant past when artists with a vision of film's possibilities shaped a new form of expression, to the immediate future, when the medium may well undergo changes as innovative as the first primitive movements.

PYRAMID ILLUSTRATED HISTORY OF THE MOVIES is a tribute to achievement: to the charismatic stars who linger in all our memories, and to the gifted people behind the cameras: the directors, the producers, the writers, the editors, the cameramen. It is also a salute to everyone who loves movies, forgives their failures, and acknowledges their shortcomings, who attends Bogart and Marx Brothers revivals and Ingmar Bergman retrospectives and festivals of forthcoming American and European films.

"The movies!" The cameras turn and the flickering images begin. And again we settle back to watch the screen, hoping to see a dream made real, an idea made palpable, or a promise fulfilled. On that unquenchable hope alone, the movies will endure.

CONTENTS

ACKNOWLEDGMENTS

I should like to thank the following people and organizations for their generous assistance in the preparation of this book: Jean Barbour, Ernest Burns, Cinemabilia, Columbia Pictures Corp., Richard Feiner and Associates, Inc., The Film and Theatre Collection at the Lincoln Center branch of the New York Public Library, Henry Kier, Jack Klaw, Paula Klaw, Alvin H. Marill, Doug McClelland, The Memory Shop, MGM, Movie Star News, Music Corporation of America, National Telefilm Associates, Inc., Paramount Pictures Corp., Premium Products, Inc., Mark Ricci, Steve Sallay, Ted Sennett, Twentieth Century-Fox, Inc., United Artists Corp., Universal Pictures Corp., Jerry Vermilye, Warner Brothers, Inc.

INTRODUCTION

Each succeeding generation somehow manages to produce its own assortment of popular heroes. Some are chosen because they have committed an act of heroism, while still others are derived from contemporary fiction or legend. For many of us, who spent a good part of our lives in the early forties watching celluloid images provide us with almost total escapism from the real world outside our favorite theaters, the hero we chose to admire and appreciate was a synthetic character created by a versatile and convincing actor, Humphrey Bogart.

Distilled from his portrayals of Sam Spade in *The Maltese Falcon* and Rick in *Casablanca,* this Bogart-created "perfect" man was a complex being whose virtues and vices tended to counterbalance each other perfectly. He was a confirmed cynic, yet compassionate enough to tolerate the weakness of others. He was moral, yet was capable of immorality within his own predetermined restrictions. He was ruggedly good-looking, but decidedly not handsome. He had his own code of ethics and he followed it to the letter, and he expected those close to him to follow it with similar dedication. He could be tough, yet he could experience the cold sweat of fear. He could be romantic, brash, insulting, clever, or any of a hundred different, equally descriptive adjectives, but when you amalgamated them all they described Humphrey Bogart, a man men wanted to emulate and women wanted to love. It was an image so strong and, apparently, so right that its appeal has transcended Bogart's own lifetime and has become a potent image for moviegoers of today and, perhaps, the future as well.

However, that was only one Bogart image. In a film career spanning twenty-six years and more than seventy-five films, there was a gallery of many different Bogart creations, some less appealing, others even surprising; we will examine this remarkable gallery in our book.

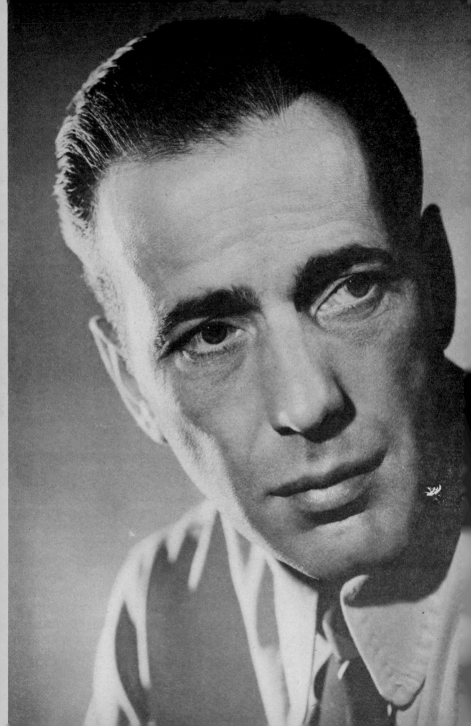

Having been exposed continuously to Bogart's cinema gallery of assorted gangsters and tough guys, one would tend to believe that his early years were difficult ones surely spawned in someplace like "Hell's Kitchen." Nothing could have been further from the truth. Bogart's parents were both extremely well-to-do, living in a fashionable West Side brownstone and being listed in that bible of snobbery, New York's *Bluebook*. His father was Dr. Belmont DeForest Bogart, a very prominent physician and surgeon, and his mother, Maude Humphrey Bogart, was a famous illustrator.

Humphrey DeForest Bogart was born on January 23, 1899, even though later publicity releases would claim that he was born on Christmas Day, 1900, to romanticize his background. Fame came to the infant early in life when his mother painted his portrait and sold it to an advertising agency. The young Bogart became known as "The Original Maude Humphrey Baby" in a promotion for a baby-food company. Although all signs point to a tranquil, though uneventful, childhood with his two younger sisters, Frances and Kay, Bogart seemed to dislike school intensely and became somewhat of a rebel. Though he was intelligent

THE MAN

and capable, he didn't seem to have the drive necessary to succeed. He barely managed to get through Trinity Grammar School and then failed at Phillips' Academy in Andover, Massachusetts, where it was hoped he would prepare himself for higher education, possibly at Yale.

Not caring to return home to live with his parents, Bogart joined the navy soon after the United States entered World War I. It was during his tour of duty on a troopship that he received a wound which gave him a permanently scarred lip and a noticeable lisp. When he returned from war duty, he went through a number of jobs until he finally sought out his boyhood friend, Bill Brady, the son of a prominent theatrical producer, William Brady, Sr., who got him varied backstage work as, among other odd jobs, a stage manager.

In 1920 he was managing a show called *Experience* and managed to get himself a two-line walk-on part. It was enough to encourage him to try acting as

11

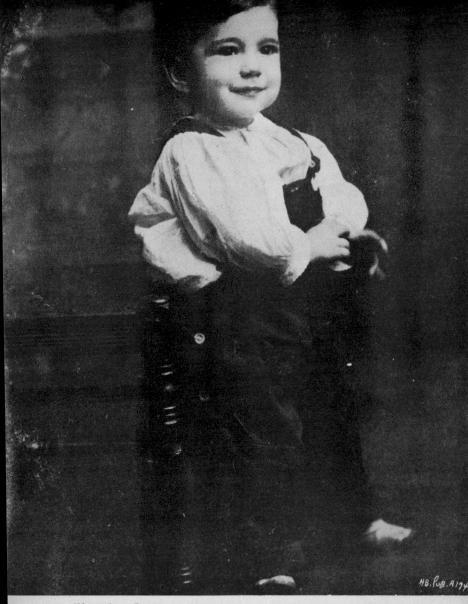

Humphrey Bogart as the child his mother painted for use in baby food advertising. Circa. 1900

a career. As road manager for the play, *The Ruined Lady,* that same year, he won his first legitimate stage role, appearing with Grace George.

In 1922 he played two parts in *Drifting* and then began a series of roles, usually appearing as a young juvenile or gadabout, in *Swifty* (1922), *Meet the Wife* (1923), *Nerves* (1924), *Hell's Bells* (1925), *Cradle Snatchers* (1925), *Baby Mine* (1927), *Saturday's Children* (1928), *Sky Rocket* (1929), and *It's a Wise Child* (1929).

It was while Bogart was appearing in *Drifting* that he first met Helen Menken, an actress of some merit, and a year later on May 20, 1926, she became his first wife. It was a stormy marriage with frequent verbal and physical battles and lasted only a year. Soon after, he met Mary Philips, another young actress he had met while appearing in *Nerves.* In May of 1928, he made her the second Mrs. Bogart.

While performing in *It's a Wise Child,* Bogart was seen by scouts from Fox Studios and was brought to Hollywood where he made a series of six films (five for Fox and one on loan-out to Universal). Unhappy with the results, he returned to do *After All* (1931). Needing money during those dollar-tight days, he

Humphrey Bogart in the navy, circa. 1918

13

again went to Hollywood and did three more bad films. Again he became disenchanted with films, vowed never to return to Hollywood again, and went back to New York to appear in *I Loved You Wednesday* (1932), *Chrysalis* (1932), *Our Wife* (1933), *The Mask and the Face* (1933), *Invitation to Murder* (1934), and finally, *The Petrified Forest* (1935), the play in which he scored an enormous success as Duke Mantee, a role he recreated in the film version. This time he decided the time was right and he remained in Hollywood, signing a long-term contract with Warner Brothers. He then began appearing in his long series of gangster portrayals. Offscreen he began to act like his screen image, acting tough and drinking more than he should.

In 1937, his wife went to Broadway to appear in *The Postman Always Rings Twice* and he started shooting *Marked Woman.* In the cast of the Bette Davis-starring film was a tough little actress named Mayo Methot. She was Bogart's equal when it came to fighting and they hit it off right away. When Mrs. Bogart returned from New York, the couple separated and in 1938 Mayo Methot became Mrs. Bogart number three. They quickly earned the nickname of "The Battling Bogarts" as they took every available opportunity to insult one another, as well as physically assault each other, especially in public. This stormy marriage lasted through Bogart's greatest film period (1938-45) as he and "Sluggy," a nickname he had given Mayo, made notorious headlines continuously, and she actually made several attempts to kill him. In spite of his explosive life offscreen, Bogart was still a conscientious actor and he always was on time for work at the studio. (As John Huston was to say in eulogizing Bogart, "Himself, he never took too seriously—his work, most seriously.") However, during the making of *Casablanca,* his wife began to cause problems. She thought he was really in love with Ingrid Bergman and she made the first of several attempts at suicide. In order to restore peace, Bogart took her with him on an extended World War II U.S.O. tour.

The making of *To Have and Have Not* finally broke up the marriage. Bogart fell in love almost immediately with his new co-star, Lauren Bacall. The days in which he was courting her turned out to be, Bogart later recalled, the happiest of his life. There was an age difference that

With Eleanor Griffith in his first important stage role: MEET THE WIFE (1923)

With Lauren Bacall and two-year-old Stephen in 1951.

presented problems—he was forty-five and she eighteen—but they overcame them and went on to have a widely publicized romance. Mayo couldn't win this battle with Bogart and on May 11, 1945, she got a Mexican divorce. She died six years later of alcoholism. On May 21, 1945, Lauren Bacall became the fourth and final Mrs. Humphrey Bogart. It was a good marriage in which two people of strong temperament succeeded in building a happy life for themselves.

In 1947, the Bogarts joined a large contingent of stars who traveled to Washington to protest the House Un-American Activities Committee's probe for Communists in the film industry. The probe resulted in the famous blacklisting of the "Hollywood Ten," all important screenwriters.

The Bogarts became more involved in politics and other pursuits. Bogart's second real love became his boat, *The Santana,* and he was aboard it as much as time would permit. Also, Bacall presented him with two children, a son, Stephen, born in 1949, and a daughter, Leslie, born in 1952. After all the years of hard living, he became a down-to-earth family man and loved every minute of it. At the same time, his screen career prospered. The Bogarts surrounded themselves with close friends (the Holmby Hills Rat Pack which included Peter Lorre, Judy Garland, Frank Sinatra, David Niven, Spencer Tracy, and Katharine Hepburn among others) and enjoyed life to its fullest. He and Bacall even did an amusing series of radio shows, including two with Bing Crosby in which Bogart actually sang, and they produced their own series for syndication called *Bold Venture,* which had a setting and atmosphere closely resembling that in *To Have and Have Not.*

While making *The Harder They Fall* in 1955, Bogart began to feel different somehow. He always seemed tired. Finally, on February 28, 1956, one of those obscure, easily overlooked notices appeared in the newspapers: "Hollywood, California. Humphrey Bogart said he would enter Good Samaritan Hospital tomorrow for surgery to remove a slight obstruction on his esophagus. The actor said the operation would be performed Thursday and that he expected to leave the hospital after about a week." Cancer was detected and in March of the same year he had an eight-hour operation which nearly cost him his life and involved the removal of a section of his esophagus. For nine months he tried to recuperate, but the disease had him beaten, even though people claimed that Bogart really believed he could lick it. On the night of January 12, 1957, instead of saying "Goodnight, kid" to Bacall, his usual line, he said "Good-bye, kid," and at two A.M. on the fourteenth, after entering a coma, Humphrey Bogart died.

In a will dated June 6, 1956, he left an estate of over a million dollars. Bacall received half and all their personal possessions, and trust funds were set up for Stephen and Leslie. A funeral service was held in All Saint's Episcopal Church in Beverly Hills on January 17 and Bogart was cremated at Forest Lawn while the service was going on. The Reverend Kermit Castellanos recited the Ten Commandments (at Bogart's request) and read Tennyson's "Crossing the Bar," a favorite of the actor's. A small scale model of *The Santana* stood on the altar rail in a glass case at Bacall's request and John Huston, one of Bogart's closest friends, delivered the eulogy before a crowd which included Gregory Peck, Gary Cooper, Marlene Dietrich, Katharine Hepburn, Jack L. Warner, Dick Powell, Nunnally Johnson, and many others. There was a minute of silence on the Warner Brothers and Twentieth Century-Fox lots.

Huston's words were a touching tribute to his old friend and he finished by saying what everyone felt deeply: "His life, though not a long one measured in years, was a rich, deep life. He got what he asked for out of life and more. He is quite irreplaceable."

Bogart's screen career falls into place as perfectly as the sequences of a good play or novel. It had a logical beginning, middle, and end which proceeded straightforwardly, something few actors could claim. Bogart went through the painstaking phases of learning his craft, of polishing his skills, of learning to act, and then progressing into a more talented performer as each succeeding year went by, until at the end he had become a thorough professional.

His first years in Hollywood were not rewarding from an acting standpoint. Since he played juvenile leads on Broadway, he was merely offered roles that used him in a similar capacity. Some roles were large, while others were merely walk-ons. However, the films did offer him an opportunity to learn the varied and complicated techniques involved in movie-making. Bogart began his first lesson in a Fox film called *A Devil With Women*.

In the thirties, most film debuts by relatively unknown stage actors who had trudged West from New York garnered little, if any, attention. Bogart was fortunate enough to be singled out by *The New York Times* critic Mordaunt Hall in his first screen endeavor:

THE EARLY FILM YEARS

"Humphrey Bogart . . . makes his debut in talking pictures and gives an ingratiating performance. Mr. Bogart is both good-looking and intelligent."

A Devil With Women (1930) fared less well. Bogart was originally brought to Hollywood to star in a Fox film called *The Man Who Came Back,* but the major role in that film was given to Charles Farrell, then one of the studio's most popular young leading men.

In *A Devil With Women,* Bogart was a rich, debonair nephew (a role consistent with the usual type of stage roles he played) of a high-ranking official in a Central American republic who spent his time getting under the skin of top-billed Victor McLaglen, who had been hired to rid the country of a notorious bandit. Both men narrowly avert being shot by a firing squad, and in an action-packed climax all ends on a happy note, with McLaglen killing the bandit and Bogart winning the girl (Mona Maris) away from the cocky Irishman. At the very least, the film was a satisfying and some-

A DEVIL WITH WOMEN (1930). With Victor McLaglen

UP THE RIVER (1930). With Spencer Tracy

what encouraging beginning for the film novice who was already making four hundred dollars a week.

Following *A Devil With Women*, Bogart appeared in *Up the River* (1930), one of the few films director John Ford would like to forget. In this inept and ludicrous comedy-melodrama, Spencer Tracy and Warren Hymer were a couple of wise-cracking convicts. Also serving a term, for accidental manslaughter, in the same prison was mild-mannered, clean-living Bogart.

When Bogart is released on a pardon, villain Morgan Wallace forces him to join in a swindle, threatening to expose his criminal past if he doesn't help. Tracy and Hymer escape and go to Bogart's assistance, returning in time to win the prison's annual baseball game. The best that can be said is that it offered Bogart a substantially large, though uninspired, role. (The film was remade in 1938, with singer Tony Martin in Bogart's role.)

His part was much shorter in his third Fox film, *Body and Soul* (1930). Aerial heroics was

his assignment this time as he portrayed, rather earnestly, an American flyer during World War I who, with two friends, is assigned to a Royal Air Force squadron in France. Married only a few days before being shipped overseas, the flyer manages to show his weaker side by picking up a new girlfriend in England. As an apparent punishment for this moral lapse, the screenwriter, Jules Furthman (who was to collaborate thirteen years later on the script for *To Have and Have Not)*, felt obliged to kill the young hero off quickly during an attack on a

BODY AND SOUL (1931). With Goodee Montgomery, Charles Farrell, and Donald Dillaway

BAD SISTER (1931). With Sidney Fox, Bette Davis, and Conrad Nagel

German observation balloon. Bogart's earlier indiscretion then complicated the remainder of the tedious plot for the film's leading man, Charles Farrell.

Another equally small and undistinguished role was given to Bogart in *Bad Sister* (1931), a film whose only real significance lies in the fact that it marked the screen debuts of two promising young actresses, Bette Davis and Sidney Fox, both of whom were to appear in future films with Bogart. *Bad Sister* was the worst kind of melodramatic drivel about the ups and downs of a spoiled merchant's daughter (Fox). Bogart was a city slicker who came to town with elaborate

A HOLY TERROR (1931). A publicity shot of Humphrey Bogart

LOVE AFFAIR (1932). With Dorothy Mackaill

plans to build a mythical factory, and who courted Fox in order to use her as a dupe in obtaining funds. Bogart ultimately left the naive young girl stranded in a cheap hotel after she had been guileless enough to run away with him. The screenplay was adapted from "The Flirt" by Booth Tarkington, an author who thrived on this soap-opera view of Americana. Fox Studios, obviously not knowing exactly what to do with Bogart, had lent him to Universal to do *Bad Sister.*

When he returned to Fox, he next found himself in a role that almost amounted to a walk-on as he made an appearance as a marine in *Women of All Nations* (1931). Victor McLaglen and Edmund Lowe were the top-billed players in this comedy-adventure as they once again played the Sergeant Flagg and Sergeant Quirt roles they had created in *What Price Glory?* and which they parlayed into a popular, though brief, series.

Bogart's final film at Fox was so uninspired and offered him so little opportunity to grow as a performer that, immediately

BIG CITY BLUES (1932). With (left to right) Inez Courtney, Evalyn Knapp, Walter Catlett, Josephine Dunn, Sheila Terry, Ned Sparks, Joan Blondell, and Lyle Talbot

after its completion, he returned to Broadway. The film, *A Holy Terror* (1931), found Bogart appearing with cowboy star George O'Brien in a minor Western about a man's pursuit of his father's killer. The trail led from the cultivated Eastern environs of polo fields to the rugged West. Bogart, completely miscast and obviously ill-at-ease, had the role of a ranch foreman who was the jealous suitor of the film's female lead, Sally Eilers.

His return to Broadway lasted only briefly and Bogart quickly bounced back to Hollywood, where he appeared in the Columbia film, *Love Affair* (1932). This film offered the actor his first important role as he received second billing to the popular leading lady, Dorothy Mackaill. Playing an aeronautical engineer who teaches a rich young heiress (Mackaill) how to fly, Bogart was fairly effective as he rapidly became party to a confusing set of in-again, out-again love affairs, made even more complex by the actions of a rival suitor and the loss of the girl's fortune. After a seemingly endless parade of complications,

Mackaill is ready to take a solo flight to oblivion, but is rescued in the proverbial "nick-of-time" by her true love, Bogart. At least it *looked* like a step upward in the struggling actor's career.

Unfortunately, success was not to be so easily attainable. He now moved from Columbia to Warner Brothers where, in his next film, he received tenth billing in *Big City Blues* (1932). In another miniscule role, Bogart was one of a group of rambunctious party-goers, which included the film's stars, Joan Blondell and Eric Linden, who ultimately find themselves embroiled in a murder. The young Bogart left his impression in this, his first film for the studio, that was to help build him into a legend, by laying fellow actor Lyle Talbot low with a well-delivered punch.

Rising director Mervyn LeRoy cast Bogart in a follow-up role at Warners in *Three On A Match* (1932), a film which is only important in the actor's career because it marked his first real attempt at portraying a tough hoodlum, here called "The

THREE ON A MATCH (1932). With Lyle Talbot, Allen Jenkins, Buster Phelps, Ann Dvorak, and Jack LaRue

MIDNIGHT (1934). With Sidney Fox

28

Mug," a role he was to find himself playing, with varying results, much too frequently over the next decade. In another awkward plot with multiple twists and connivances involving the film's three leading ladies—Joan Blondell, Ann Dvorak, and Bette Davis—Bogart was hired by Lyle Talbot to kidnap a young boy in order to obtain ransom enough to pay off the latter's excessive gambling debts. Bogart really had so little to do that he once again decided to desert films and he retreated to the relative safety of his old standby, the Broadway theater.

For the next four years, Bogart was to continue to gain experience and grow as an actor on Broadway, taking time out only once to appear in *Midnight* (1934) as a gangster who is killed by leading lady Sidney Fox when he spurns her. It did little to advance his stature as a film actor, and Bogart always regretted making this trivial sojourn.

After having made ten totally inconsequential movies, Bogart announced that it would really take something very important to get him to ever return to Hollywood again. This important item turned out to be his appearance as Duke Mantee in *The Petrified Forest*.

The second phase of Bogart's screen career was more rewarding financially, but hardly noteworthy for his continued growth as a performer. He was to be unmercifully type-cast as a gangster, with few chances to break out of the mold. Five solid years were spent with guns, molls, tough-talk, and getting killed before the end credits, but Bogart tolerated all of it, feeling along with most good actors that you learn acting by acting and if you're good, and patient, your chance will come. He polished his characterization by making his gangsters the idols of all gangsters: sneering, unfeeling, unreasoning, brutal, and totally irredeemable—all variations on a theme introduced with *The Petrified Forest.*

Broadway producer Arthur Hopkins had gotten Bogart the part of Duke Mantee in *The Petrified Forest* in spite of objections from the play's author, Robert Sherwood, that he wasn't right for the role. Bogart proved the author wrong and Leslie Howard, who had the leading role, liked Bogart's performance so much that he promised him that if the play was ever brought to the screen he would see that Bogart recreated his stage role. It was a promise Howard kept. Warner Brothers had already

DUKE MANTEE AND COMPANY

penciled in Edward G. Robinson for the part, but Howard refused to do the film without Bogart, forcing the studio to give in. Directed by Archie Mayo, *The Petrified Forest* (1936) gave a tremendous boost to Bogart's screen career by providing him with a ready-made showcase for his talent. The movie was a very faithful adaptation of the play as it told of a group of diverse personalities who find themselves held at bay in a small service-station-restaurant by a ruthless gunman and his gang on the run from pursuing police. There were heavily symbolic overtones involving the overrunning of the doomed intellectuals by corruptive brute force. (Bogart's later *Key Largo,* also adapted from a play, bore many close similarities to this film.)

Into this seemingly fragile framework, the screenplay by Charles Kenyon and Delmer Daves weaves a tapestry of penetrating character studies. First there is Alan Squier (Leslie Howard), a disillusioned writer and intellectual who realizes he is a member of a vanishing breed of men whose visions of a Utopian existence have given way to the harsh realities of a world that no longer has any room for his type of dreamer. Frustrated and quietly despairing, he meets a dreamer of another type, Gaby Maple (Bette Davis). She shares Squier's love of beauty and poetry and dreams of fleeing her stifling entrapment at the restaurant and traveling to France. Into their world of fanciful idealism enters Duke Mantee (Bogart)—the reality, the brute force which threatens not only the dreamers but all of society. It is a finely honed portrait of ultimate evil, magnificently played by Bogart with all the sneering, uncompromising ferocity the role demanded. It was one of Bogart's finest portrayals and it was the model, although consi-

THE PETRIFIED FOREST (1936). With Bette Davis and Leslie Howard

THE PETRIFIED FOREST (1936). Rare production shot with (left to right) Bette Davis, Leslie Howard, Dick Foran, Slim Thompson, Joseph Sawyer, director Archie Mayo (in white shirt), and Charley Grapewin (seated far right)

derably restrained, he would follow for the next five years or so of his career. Approximately twenty years later, on May 30, 1955, Bogart recreated his original role in a television production of *The Petrified Forest*. Directed by Delbert Mann, the play featured Lauren Bacall in the Davis role and Henry Fonda in Howard's part. After all those years, Bogart still had the character down perfectly and received excellent notices.

Following his animalistic portrayal in *The Petrified Forest*, Bogart became a much more articulate and calculating killer in his second film of the year, *Bullets or Ballots* (1936), a slickly produced entertainment starring Edward G. Robinson as a crusading crime-buster, modeled after true-life cop Johnny

Broderick, known as "the toughest cop on Broadway," who pretended to be thrown off the police force in order to infiltrate Bogart's gang and get the evidence to bring him to justice. Bogart was generally poker-faced as he went about his gun-happy chores of eliminating a respected newspaperman as well as his partner-in-crime, Barton MacLane, in a typically Bogartian double-cross. The exciting finale found both Bogart and Robinson cutting each other down with blazing guns, an unusual ending for this period in film history, but one which Robinson had fought hard to retain. The film was a typical Warners' gangland melodrama, but William Keighley directed it with crisp efficiency.

Critics claimed that Bogart's next film, *Two Against the World* (1936), a decidedly inferior remake of *Five Star Final* (1931), featured some of the most juvenile dialogue to ever come out of Hollywood. It was

TWO AGAINST THE WORLD (1936). With Beverly Roberts

CHINA CLIPPER (1936). With Pat O'Brien

BLACK LEGION (1937). A highlight
of this film was the depiction of
vigilante rituals.

hard to refute the claim as film-goers watched Bogart portray a radio-station manager who was disgusted with the muckraking broadcast policies of his bosses, particularly after one extremely sordid revelation causes a highly respected married couple to commit suicide. Bogart expressed his contempt in more functional terms by cooperating with the Radio Commission to "clean up the airwaves." There was little chance for Bogart to do anything but appear forthright and determined as he plowed through another of Jack Warner's bread-and-butter programmers.

Bogart temporarily left the field of crime to portray a more respectable type in his subsequent effort, *China Clipper* (1936). On its simplest level *China Clipper* relates a routine story of an airline owner's (Pat O'Brien) desire to put into operation a trans-Pacific airline. Soap-opera dramatics take over quickly as O'Brien's dedication to his project costs him his wife, his friends, and the clichéd obligatory, for this genre, death of an elderly associate designer. Bogart's undistinguished role was that of a wise-cracking pilot, frequently engaging in verbal sparring with O'Brien and fellow pilot Ross Alexander, who even-

tually makes the record-breaking flight across the Pacific in the film's finale. *China Clipper* is merely artificial drama, but it has a certain value for its generally well-integrated use of newsreel and stock shots of the actual China Clippers in operation. One particularly exciting shot is of the mammoth plane flying over an as-yet-uncompleted Golden Gate Bridge with its gigantic opposing spans reaching out into empty air, waiting patiently for its final connecting links.

Sporting a pencil-line mustache, Bogart was grossly victimized by studio casting in his next film, *Isle of Fury* (1936), an incredibly inept vehicle that found him playing a fugitive hiding out on a South Sea island. Tracking him down was stalwart Donald Woods who gives up the quest, after complications that included his love affair with Bogart's wife (Margaret Lindsay), thwarted when he learns that Bogart has completely reformed and is leading a happily married life. (The film was a remake of *The Narrow Corner* filmed by Warner Brothers in 1933.) When asked about this film, Bogart always claimed wishfully, no doubt, that he couldn't remember even making it.

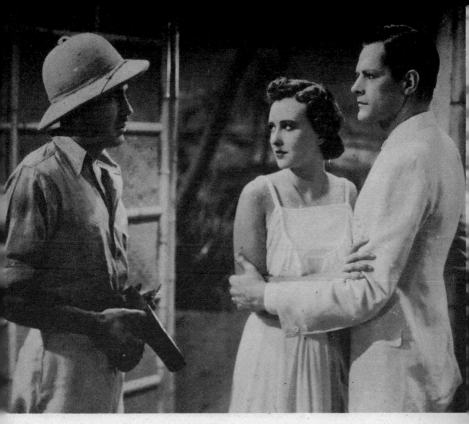

ISLE OF FURY (1936). With Margaret Lindsay and Donald Woods

Black Legion (1937), Bogart's first film of the year, was editorial cinema of the first order and gave the actor his first chance to play a character with real dimension since *The Petrified Forest.* Somewhat paralleling documentary evidence given by the executioner of a vigilante group that had terrorized the Midwest in 1935 and 1936, the film was an uncompromisingly brutal portrait of the ruthlessness of vigilante mob action. Bogart had a most difficult acting assignment, that of a factory worker who becomes disenchanted when he loses out on an important job promotion and joins a hooded gang of "pro-American" malcontents (whose grotesque initiation rites are a frightening visual highlight) to gain retaliation. Bogart's gradual moral disintegration as he becomes more and more involved

BLACK LEGION (1937). With Helen Flint and Joseph Sawyer

in the illicit organization (to the point where he actually kills his best friend) was a small-scale forerunner of the type of mental deterioration he was to later polish and perfect in *The Treasure of the Sierra Madre* and *The Caine Mutiny*. Under Archie Mayo's direction, Bogart interpreted the screenplay by Abem Finkel and William Wister Haines in an exemplary manner as he turned from a quiet,

loving family man to a desperate human being.

The Great O'Malley (1937), directed by William Dieterle, was Bogart's second film with Pat O'Brien, a man he deeply respected as a person and as an actor. In this very predictable programmer, O'Brien was an overofficious cop whose adherence to the letter of the law alienates friends as well as foes. Bogart was an honest family man who was forced to turn to crime in order to provide for his family after O'Brien arrested him for a petty offense and caused him to lose a job opportunity. Bogart had an excellent chance to show some versatility by turning from his earlier carefree, attitude into one of frustration and bitter hatred, and he carried it off rather effectively.

A much needed change of pace for Bogart took place in his next film, *Marked Woman* (1937). This time, in a blistering melodrama directed by Lloyd Bacon, he played the role of a good guy, a racket-busting district attorney out to snare a night-club owner (Eduardo Ciannelli) who

THE GREAT O'MALLEY (1937). With Frieda Inescort, Pat O'Brien, and Sybil Jason

MARKED WOMAN (1937) With Bette Davis, Mayo Methot (Bogart's third wife), and Rosalind Marquis

was exploiting his "hostesses," one of whom was the film's leading lady, Bette Davis, in a role she fought very hard with studio heads to get after a long series of poor melodramas. Bogart's performance successfully blended rugged determination and calmly exhibited compassion and concern. He was particularly effective, both crisp and penetrating, in his courtroom scenes, which served as an early warmup for similar duty a decade later in *Knock On Any Door*. Mayo Methot was also in the cast as one of the hostesses and it was during the filming that Bogart took her as his second wife.

Not satisfied with having massacred each other in *Bullets or Ballots* a year earlier, Bogart was rematched with Edward G. Robinson in a fast-moving boxing drama, *Kid Galahad* (1938). Robinson was a tough manager who discovers, quite by accident, a young bellhop (Wayne Morris) with a punch he feels is strong enough to win a championship for him. (This film was retitled *The Battling Bellhop* for television so as to not confuse it with the much later, and inferior, remake starring Elvis Presley.) When the fighter falls for his sister (Jane Bryan), Robinson decides to double-cross him and arranges a bout with a tough opponent he feels will beat the kid to pieces. Bogart, grim and self-serving, was the malevolent gangster-manager of the tough opponent and, when Robinson has a change of heart through the intercession of his mistress (Bette Davis) and helps the kid win, he and Bogart again wind up slaughtering each other in a hail of bullets.

Bogart returned quickly to a life of crime in his next film, *San Quentin* (1937), the movie which provided the pattern from which almost all of the actor's subsequent prison dramas were to be cut. Bogart, trying vainly to add some depth and meaning to a role which offered little of either, was a convicted robber sent to San Quentin and assigned to a road gang as a rehabilatative step instituted by the prison yard captain, Pat O'Brien. When Bogart is maliciously informed, through the efforts of perennially bad Barton MacLane, that O'Brien has less than honorable intentions toward his sister, Ann Sheridan, he breaks out and shoots O'Brien, though not seriously. When he finds that he has erred, he decides to give himself up, but is shot as he is returning. As he staggers up to the prison gates, dying, he pleads for his fellow prisoners to cooperate with O'Brien. *San Quentin*, though far from one of Bogart's best roles, is almost always included in his film retrospectives as a favorite choice of his fans.

Bogart's next appearance was much more rewarding. *Dead End* (1937) turned out to be his most important film since *The Petrified Forest*. A highly successful play by Sidney Kingsley, *Dead End* was adapted for the screen by fellow playwright, Lillian Hellman. In a brilliantly executed New York slum setting photographed by Gregg Toland, it offered a vivid portrait of people caught up in a constant struggle to somehow fulfill themselves despite the oppressive environment that seemed to stifle their every attempt. Joel McCrea was a frustrated architect who dreamed of tearing down the slums and Sylvia Sidney portrayed a shopgirl striving for identity and meaning in her life, a life made even more com-

SAN QUENTIN (1937). With Pat O'Brien

plicated by having to look after her brother (Billy Halop). The boy idolizes the decadent Bogart, an adulation shared by the rest of the Dead End Kids, here recreating their original Broadway roles with rowdy good humor. Opposing these idealists is their (and society's) real threat, Bogart, a swaggering braggart and killer named Baby Face Martin. Bogart is rebuffed by a mother (Marjorie Main) who abhors him and an ex-girlfriend (Claire Trevor) who leaves him bitter and disillusioned when he finds that she has become a prostitute. Rebuked by those he had been sentimental enough to want to visit, he quickly reverts to type and plans a kidnaping in order to salvage something from the wasted affair. He nearly kills McCrea before he is himself killed when his plans go awry. Director William Wyler obtained a searing, provocative performance from Bogart, proving that the actor was capable of handling difficult material with considerable skill. *Dead End* remains a probing, soul-wrenching screen experience and is one of Bogart's best films.

Unfortunately, superlatives were not in order for his final film of the year. *Stand-In* (1937) gave Bogart his first real chance to play comedy as it matched him once again with Leslie Howard, *The Petrified Forest* co-star,

DEAD END (1937). With Marjorie Main

DEAD END (1937). With Joel McCrea and Allen Jenkins

SWING YOUR LADY (1938). With Allen Jenkins, Frank McHugh, and Nat Pendleton

in a mildly amusing tale of an efficiency expert (Howard) who is sent to Hollywood to save a faltering studio from potential ruin. Howard was appropriately stuffy as he enlisted the aid of former child star Joan Blondell to teach him the more practical side of movie-making. Bogart was a producer-editor who had taken to the bottle after an unsuccessful romance with one of the studio's stars, but snaps out of his lethargy when Howard

uses him to salvage a movie "bomb" and turn it into a success big enough to save the studio. Bogart drew his share of laughs, but the movie hardly seemed worth the effort. It was Bogart's second loan-out in a row from Warner Brothers, *Stand-In* being released, as was *Dead End,* by United Artists.

Bogart's first film for 1938 was a sorry vehicle called *Swing Your Lady* (1938). A cheap, contemptible attempt to cash in on

CRIME SCHOOL (1938). With (left to right) Bernard Punsley, Gabriel Dell, Huntz Hall, Bobby Jordan, Leo Gorcey, Billy Halop, and director Lewis Seiler.

rustic humor, it found Bogart playing a fast-buck promoter who goes to the Ozarks with a dumb wrestler (Nat Pendleton) and sets up an incredible match with a town Amazon (Louise Fazenda). Pendleton falls for the lady and refuses to fight her. Bogart, needing money, arranges a grudge match between his man and the female giant's jealous suitor. Quite naturally, true love triumphs as Pendleton wins and gets the hand of his newfound love interest. Prominent in the cast were the Weavers, a hillbilly family who later went on to a series of low-budget features for Republic, and Penny Singleton, who achieved fame (and screen misfortune because of the typecasting) as comic-strip heroine "Blondie" in a long series of comedies turned out by Columbia. As far as Bogart was concerned, the whole effort was tasteless and vulgar and he considered it his worst film performance.

Bogart was back in prison in

CRIME SCHOOL (1938). With Weldon Heyburn and Cy Kendall

MEN ARE SUCH FOOLS (1938). With Priscilla Lane

his next screen appearance. *Crime School* (1938) was clearly from the same mold as *San Quentin* and Cagney's *The Mayor of Hell.* With the Dead End Kids a money-making property after *Dead End,* it seemed a natural exploitative move to team them again with Bogart in hopes of a similar big payoff. The result was a mediocre film in which Bogart played, in a drab, unemotional style, a deputy commissioner of correction who takes over the running of a reformatory housing the Kids when he finds the superintendent is a sadist. There is a threat to Bogart's plan when the Kids escape as part of the superintendent's calculated attempt to prove Bogart's regenerative prison policies are valueless, but the ruse fails as Bogart gets the boys back and wins the customary accolades.

Men Are Such Fools (1938), his next film, was another disappointing effort. The best review of this dreary, trifling film was a comment in *The New York Times:* "For the benefit of those who like to know what a picture is about, we can only say that *Men Are Such Fools* is about an hour too long." Most Bogart fans would agree, as they found him woodenly playing an advertising executive involved in a fatuous love triangle, with leading lady Priscilla Lane using him as a pawn to make Wayne Morris jealous. *Men Are Such Fools* was stiffly directed by Busby Berkeley in one of his few attempts at non-musical comedy.

Bogart vulgarly referred to *The Amazing Dr. Clitterhouse* (1938) as "The Amazing Dr. Clitoris" (an obvious display of contempt for a film in which he played a thief called "Rocks" Valentine). In the role played by Cedric Hardwicke in Barré Lyndon's stage play, Edward G. Robinson was top-billed as a psychologist writing a book on the physiological reactions of criminals. Wanting firsthand experience, he becomes a jewel thief and eventually works his way into a gang headed by Bogart. Bogart immediately resents Robinson's presence and sets up a scheme to force the doctor to rob his wealthy friends. Robinson, needing a chapter on homicide for his thesis, responds by poisoning Bogart and then calmly studies him as he dies. Robinson is then caught and, in an incredible finale, is paradoxically acquitted. Bogart's grimacing performance was patently unnoteworthy. The screenplay for *The Amazing Dr. Clitterhouse* was co-authored by John Wexley and a writer who was to play an im-

THE AMAZING DR. CLITTERHOUSE (1938). With Maxie Rosenbloom, Edward G. Robinson, and Claire Trevor

portant role in Bogart's subsequent career, John Huston.

During the thirties one of the nation's greatest heroes was the crusading district attorney in New York City, Thomas E. Dewey. With almost daily headlines proclaiming his relentless pursuit of bigtime racketeers, it was only natural that the movie studios, who tried to exploit topical themes whenever possible, would find some way to fashion movies to parallel Dewey's criminal clean-up. It was hardly surprising, then, to find not one but two minor melodramas appearing within a single week in late 1938 which featured crusading district attorneys bent on deli-

ANGELS WITH DIRTY FACES (1938). With James Cagney

vering fast, tough justice to the "Kingpins of Crime."

The lesser of the two films was a routine programmer from RKO called *Smashing the Rackets*, starring Chester Morris. Warner Brothers was much better equipped for this kind of subject. Their *Racket Busters* (1938) was an exciting tale of gangsters who moved in on Manhattan's trucking business. Heading the mob, naturally, was Bogart in his now-stereotyped role as the wooden-faced, unfeeling hood. Opposing the so-called Protective Association was George Brent, whose oldest friend is murdered because he dared testify against the mob. Brent finally leads the truckers in a fist-swinging revolt against their predators. In order to tie the whole thing in with Dewey, the studio gave the role of special prosecutor to Walter Abel, an actor who bore an uncanny resemblance to the young crime fighter.

Bogart closed out the third year of his Warners' contract with one of his most-remembered films. *Angels With Dirty Faces* (1938) has become a favorite Bogart film by default; it has been shown so often and has served as the prime source of material for countless satirists and impressionists. Written for the screen by John Wexley and Warren Duff, the now overly familiar tale of the two young boys who grow up to be on opposing sides of the fence—one a gangster (James Cagney) and the

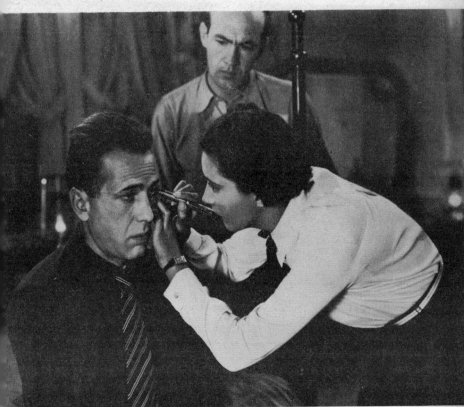

KING OF THE UNDERWORLD (1939). With Elliott Sullivan and Kay Francis

57

THE OKLAHOMA KID (1939). As Whip McCord

other a priest (Pat O'Brien)—was blatantly sentimental. Its saving virtues were the performances by the leads, slick, rapid-fire direction by Michael Curtiz, a good music score by Max Steiner, and superior art direction by Robert Hass. Bogart had little, and certainly nothing new, to do as he played Cagney's lawyer - turned - nightclub - owner who double-crosses him and gets shot, once again, for his duplicity. Cagney was sent to the chair and O'Brien asked him as a final favor to forsake his bravado and turn cowardly to prevent the Dead End Kids from continuing to idolize him as a hero. The film ends with O'Brien asking the Kids to join him in a prayer "for a boy who couldn't run as fast as I could." Pure hokum to be sure, but still entertaining as a prototype of its genre.

Not even the presence of the redoubtable Kay Francis in the cast could save Bogart's next film, *King of the Underworld* (1939), from being another film the actor thoroughly disliked. This time, as a criminal with de-

THE OKLAHOMA KID (1939). With Ward Bond

DARK VICTORY (1939). With Bette Davis

lusions of grandeur, he was featured prominently in the usual murders and wanton pillage. An incredible finale found Bogart and his men being temporarily blinded by Francis, playing a doctor, and chasing her and co-star James Stephenson about their hideout, trying to kill them before the police arrive. Bogart, overly made-up and pouting continuously, was acting at his unemotional zenith as he once

again was cut down by the law.

It had been eight years since Bogart fared badly in his first cowboy role *(A Holy Terror)* and now he was given a second chance to prove himself in the saddle as James Cagney's nemesis in *The Oklahoma Kid* (1939). He obviously hadn't learned his lesson as he gave an equally unconvincing performance as an outlaw gang leader who deceitfully obtains saloon and gam-

*YOU CAN'T GET AWAY WITH MURDER (1939). With Joseph Crehan
Billy Halop and Joseph King*

bling rights in return for letting Cagney's father and brother have rights to a site on which they plan to build a town. Later, Cagney's father is lynched after being jailed in a frame-up by Bogart. Cagney ultimately gets revenge, but not until the finale begins to look like the last act of *Hamlet* with bodies scattered all over the prairie. Dressed in an all-black outfit, Bogart looked the very model of Western villainy, but he destroyed the image entirely when he opened his mouth or leaped onto a horse. As one reviewer commented: "Another authentic Westerner—from Tenth Avenue!"

As evidence that it is much better to be type-cast than miscast, witness Bogart in *Dark Victory* (1939), his third film of the year at Warners. The movie, one of Bette Davis's most memorable and popular successes, was a highly emotional tear-jerker that in less capable hands might have spelled disaster. Playing a wild, free-living heiress who learns that she has a malignant brain tumor, Davis endowed scene after scene with the special magic only she was capable of conjuring. Swept into the current of events was Bogart playing an Irish groom, with an accent that must have had Pat O'Brien cringing, who fails in an attempt to make love to her, yet encourages her to enjoy what time she has left with her true love, George Brent. Uneasy and unconvincing in the role, Bogart must indeed have felt like an unsightly blemish marring a thing of beauty when he viewed his performance in this film.

For a studio that had specialized in criminal mayhem for a decade, *You Can't Get Away With Murder* (1939) seemed a somewhat ironic title for Warner Brothers to tag on to Bogart's next factory-produced prison melodrama. In this one Bogart was a stone-faced, unfeeling penny-ante crook who led Dead End Kid Billy Halop into a life of crime. When a killing results from a robbery and an innocent man is convicted, Bogart forces Halop to remain silent. Later, when they find themselves in prison, Bogart senses the kid is weakening and plans a breakout, hoping to kill Halop in the confusion. The breakout fails, but Bogart does kill Halop, but not before he clears the innocent victim and sends Bogart to a well-deserved fate in the "hot seat."

His next film proved to be an enjoyable melodrama. After nearly a decade of concentrating on the gangster period of the twenties, it appeared that Warner Brothers had decided to

THE ROARING TWENTIES (1939). With James Cagney

make one final glorified kiss-off to the genre in the spectacularly staged *The Roaring Twenties* (1939). All the time-tested ploys were in evidence as director Raoul Walsh, producer Hal Wallis, and writers Jerry Wald, Richard Macaulay, and Robert Rossen (working from a Mark Hellinger story) fashioned a film containing every possible cliché connected with the era. The tone of the piece was set immediately by Mark Hellinger himself as he pompously intoned as narrator, "This film is a memory . . . and I am grateful for it." The story revolved about three war buddies (Cagney, Bogart, and Jeffrey Lynn) who return to civilian life and find little in the way of

job opportunities available. Lynn decides to be come a lawyer while Cagney and Bogart build up separate profitable bootlegging businesses. The twists of plot find Cagney's fortunes falling as Bogart's rise, with the two competing to control the rackets. Cagney is reduced to a pathetic (even laughable) figure driving a cab and wearing rags.

Bogart's portrayal was interesting as we watched him coldly murder an ex-army sergeant who had given him a rough time in the service, and then set out to get rid of Lynn, now a successful lawyer working for the district attorney and intent on crushing Bogart's empire. In the final

THE ROARING TWENTIES (1939).
With James Cagney

THE RETURN OF DOCTOR X (1939). As Marshall Quesne, alias the Mysterious Doctor Xavier

THE RETURN OF DOCTOR X (1939). With Dennis Morgan and John Litel

scenes, Bogart goes through a remarkable number of facial expressions as he turns from a smiling, swaggering top-dog ordering Cagney to be taken for a ride into a sniveling, pleading coward begging for his life as Cagney escapes from his armed guard, grabs a gun, and pumps numerous bullets into him. The film closes with an overtheatrical sequence where Cagney, mortally wounded in a shootout with Bogart's surviving henchmen, staggers in his , rubber-legged fashion to the steps of a snow-covered church, finally collapses, and dies as Gladys George, playing Cagney's loyal old friend, delivers his memorable epitaph: "He used to be a big shot!" *The Roaring Twenties* was one of Warner's most commercially successful films of the year and remains good, though admittedly corny, screen entertainment.

Jack Warner had the nasty habit of punishing errant actors (those who had the audacity to rebel against bad scripts and

INVISIBLE STRIPES (1939). With William Holden and George Raft

who wanted salary increases) with ghastly two-bit films like *The Return of Doctor X* (1939). Bogart fell easy victim to his childish vengeance. In this futile attempt to cash in on the success of the studio's earlier horror classic, *Doctor X* (1932), Bogart was an executed murderer who was brought back to life to finish his existence as a vampire. Wearing pasty-faced make-up and a white streak in his hair, he was absolutely ludicrous as he smirked through scene after scene seeking to drain Type-One blood from a bevy of studio starlets in this journey into complete tastelessness.

Invisible Stripes (1939), Bogart's last film of the year placed him back in the underworld. Even though the movie boasted a superior cast headed by George Raft, William Holden, Flora Robson, and Jane Bryan, it was still no more than a routine crime drama that found Raft and Bogart as criminal cohorts who make the mistake of antagonizing their former gang members, who then shoot them both down in the film's gun-happy climax. Playing Raft's in-genuous brother in one of his first films, Holden showed he had a lot to learn, while Bogart showed that he had already learned all he could about his type of role. In his *New York Times* review, B. R. Crisler noted that Bogart played his "customary role of the Crook They Couldn't Crack with Kindness."

Virginia City (1940) was Bogart's first released film of the forties and his final appearance in a Western. Colorfully directed by Michael Curtiz, it was an expensively mounted but rather routinely scripted tale of a Union Army officer (Errol Flynn) who blocks the plan of his Rebel antagonist (Randolph Scott) to ship five million dollars in gold to aid the Confederacy. Bogart, again sporting his unappealing mustache, was a half-breed outlaw hired by Scott to divert Flynn but who finds the temptation of having the money for himself irresistible, a decision which eventually costs him his life. Not only was Bogart forced to play a poorly delineated role in *Virginia City,* but he was required to work with Flynn and Scott, two actors for whom

he had a tremendous personal dislike.

Both George Raft and John Garfield had turned down the lead role in *It All Came True* (1940) and Bogart won it by default. In this comedy-drama directed by Lewis Seiler, Bogart was a fugitive killer who hid out in a rundown boarding house harboring a collection of talented amateur performers and maternally oriented older women. Bogart convinces them to convert the place into a night club and on opening night he is caught by the police, clearing an innocent man (Jeffrey Lynn) of suspicion in the murder he had actually committed. Bogart was evidently having a good time as he delivered such lines as: "I hate mothers: all this silver-threads among the gold stuff!" and had a very funny scene where he is "mothered" by Una O'Connor and Jessie Busley. However, *The New York Times'* critic, B. R. Crisler, summed up the film correctly when he said that *It All Came True* went "from simple to simple-minded."

Warner Brothers let Edward G. Robinson play the title role in *Dr. Ehrlich's Magic Bullet* on the condition that he enact one more gangster role, and the result, *Brother Orchid* (1940) was

VIRGINIA CITY (1940). With George Regas, Moroni Olsen, and Paul Fix

IT ALL CAME TRUE (1940). With Jessie Busley, Grant Mitchell, Brandon Tynan, and ZaSu Pitts

a pleasant comedy-drama. Robinson played a gangster whose gang Bogart wanted to take over. He survives Bogart's murder attempt and finds sanctuary in a monastary where he learns to cultivate flowers. When Bogart muscles in on the monastary's flower business, Robinson rounds up a group of friends and breaks up Bogart's gang. Bogart was at his peak as a hood who behaved like a Cheshire cat, smilingly agreeing with Robinson all the while he was planning to do away with him. Lloyd Bacon directed with restraint, never letting Bogart's viciousness exceed the limits allowable for comedy.

Bogart had an opportunity for considerably more self-expression in his next screen role in *They Drive By Night* (1941), a film which has remained popular with audiences not so much for its story, which is rather trivial, but for the forceful performances contributed by all its leading players—George Raft, Ann Sheridan, Ida Lupino, and Bogart—fast-paced direction by Raoul Walsh, and a crackling script by Jerry Wald and Richard Macaulay. Raft and Bogart were brothers who wanted to start their own trucking business and eventually succeed, but not before Bogart loses an arm in an accident and Lupino nearly sends Raft to jail for a murder she committed. (The trial sequence in which her latent insanity causes her to disintegrate into hysterics on the witness stand is one of the screen's best-remembered moments.) Bogart was convincing as his earlier wisecracking gave way to the frustrations and bitterness of a cripple and then back again to resigned complacency as he accepted the role life had given him to play out.

It is not always easy to get audiences to accept the ennoble-ment of a gangster without reservation, but in *High Sierra* (1941), Bogart's second film of the year, the task was handled more than satisfactorily. George Raft, Edward G. Robinson, James Cagney, and Paul Muni had all turned down the leading role of killer-on-the-run Roy Earle, and the part went to Bogart, who seldom turned down anything as most of his earlier roles attest. The decision was a wise one, for *High Sierra* was the film that changed the course of Bogart's career and boosted him to stardom.

As Earle, Bogart was expanding on the criminal characterization he had already mastered in a dozen earlier films, giving it greater depth by adding contrasting elements of warmth and compassion to offset the dominant violence. (He helps a club-footed girl, Velma [Joan Leslie], who repays him only with contempt and indifference.) Though the role was essentially another step in Warners' defanging and sentimentalizing of the gangster that had started with *Angels With Dirty Faces,* Bogart's interpretation already showed signs of the special qualities that were to become an important part of his mystique in a few more films. Here, for the first time, was the Bogartian man

THEY DRIVE BY NIGHT (1940). With Ann Sheridan and George Raft

outside society's laws who had his own private sense of loyalty, integrity, and honor. His death even takes on an heroic dimension as he is shot down from his lofty perch atop a mountain, after showing concern for a pet dog as a final memorable kindness. Bogart's performance turns *High Sierra* into an elegiac film.

As a film, *High Sierra* has

THEY DRIVE BY NIGHT (1940). As Paul Fabrini.

HIGH SIERRA (1941). With Ida Lupino

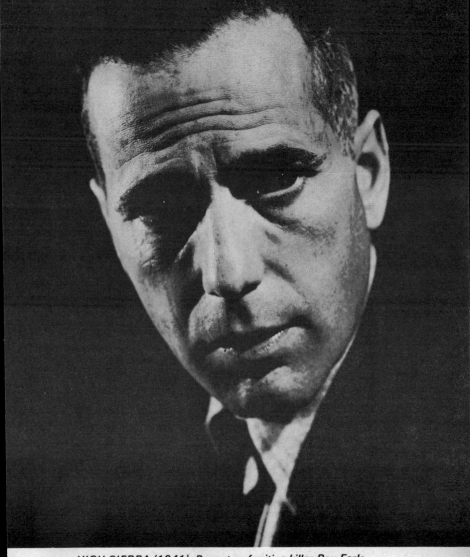

HIGH SIERRA (1941). Bogart as fugitive killer Roy Earle

HIGH SIERRA (1941). With Arthur Kennedy, Ida Lupino, and Alan Curtis

other notable qualities, particularly Ida Lupino's strong and moving performance as Marie, the girl who brings out Roy Earle's more human emotions. The movie was remade as a Western, *Colorado Territory* (1949), and as *I Died a Thousand Times* (1955), with Jack Palance and Shelley Winters in the Bogart and Lupino roles. Neither came up to the stylish treatment given *High Sierra* by director Raoul

Walsh from an exceptionally good script by John Huston and W. R. Burnett. This film is a special favorite, and deservedly so, with most Bogart fans.

Although enormous success was only one more film away, Bogart still had to appear in *The Wagons Roll At Night* (1941), a film important to the actor only in that he received top-star billing for the first time, something he was never to lose for the re-

THE WAGONS ROLL AT NIGHT (1941). With Sylvia Sidney

mainder of his career. Bogart personally referred to the film as "that one I made after *High Sierra,*" finding the title difficult to remember and caring little for the film itself. It was an accurate appraisal, for the film was nothing more than a remake of *Kid Galahad*, with the hero (Eddie Albert) as a lion tamer instead of a boxer. Bogart walked listlessly through his role as the owner of the traveling carnival who heroically gives up his life to save Albert's. Sylvia Sidney appeared in the Bette Davis role as Bogart's troubled girlfriend, a fortuneteller with the carnival. The film was a very disappointing follow-up to Bogart's triumph in *High Sierra*, but better things lay immediately ahead.

Having finally worked his way into becoming a top-billed star, Bogart was now ready for the

THE
PEAK YEARS

third stage of his career. Success was now his, and it was a time of immense satisfaction for the actor who had spent a decade preparing for it. He was now top-dog, taking second place to no other actor. All the good roles and the acceptance and adulation of the public were his and he relished every delicious moment of it as he set about creating the famous Bogart image, an image which was to dominate the screen for the next six years, an image which found its basic construction in *The Maltese Falcon*.

Bogart was to say many times in later years that there were few things about which he could feel proud, but that *The Maltese Falcon* (1941) was one of them. He had every right to feel that way about the film for it is that rarest of Hollywood commodities, a nearly flawless film masterpiece. Director John Huston was always to credit Bogart's performance for the film's success, but most people acknowledge the fact that Huston's script and electric direction were major contributions. Amazingly, it was Huston's first directorial effort and there are many who feel it remains his *best* film. As

the author of the screenplay, Huston made every effort to do justice, and remain faithful, to Dashiell Hammett's novel. Failure to maintain integrity with the original source was the primary reason two earlier versions, *The Maltese Falcon* (1931) with Ricardo Cortez and Bebe Daniels (retitled *Dangerous Lady* for television prints) and *Satan Met a Lady* (1936) with Warren William and Bette Davis, had failed. However, in remaining faithful, the newest version asked audiences to accept the complicated plot at its full strength and that is where the film's main flaw occurs. Names, murders, and intrigues turn up so quickly that it is extremely difficult to understand exactly what is happening in this tale of an assortment of characters in search of a fabulous jewel-encrusted falcon.

In spite of the expertise behind the camera, including Arthur Edeson's low-key photography and Thomas Richards' efficient editing, it is the memorable characterizations on the screen that really stand out.

THE MALTESE FALCON (1941). With Mary Astor

Probably in no other film will a viewer find a collection of such diverse human beings whose perfectly constructed portrayals remain permanently locked in one's memory. Mary Astor's Brigid O'Shaughnessy is a striking picture of feminine deceit and betrayal. Able to shed tears on command, she is a confirmed liar who can be tough as nails when the occasion demands; she can make passionate love to Bogart, but wouldn't hesitate a moment to kill him if it suited her plan. Her reactions to Bogart at the film's conclusion—first of fear, then hatred, and finally resignation as Bogart tells her, "You killed Miles and you're going over for it"—are fascinating to watch and her performance is surely one of the screen's most brilliant portrayals of duplicity masked with allure. Sydney Greenstreet, in his movie debut, was equally memorable as the bloated Kasper Gutman, the man behind the search for the elusive black bird, and almost stole the picture. Cunning, determined, appreciative of the finer things in life, he is a man who would devote his entire life to a single quest if need be. Huston accentuated his dominating bulk by shooting him from low angles, allowing him to completely monopolize certain key scenes.

Peter Lorre's Joel Cairo was a resolute picture of classic effeminacy. With curled hair and immaculate, fastidious dress, he is an awkward and unpredictable accomplice of Greenstreet. At one moment he is a quiet picture of timidity, and the next he is lashing out with verbal vehemence at the Fat Man. Even minor roles are perfectly chosen: Elisha Cook, Jr., as the epitome of the pulp fiction "gunsel," uttering comic-strip dialogue as he hides behind the safety of his oversized forty-five caliber automatic; Jerome Cowan as Bogart's down-to-earth partner, a man Bogart would be willing to risk his life for if the situation demanded; and Ward Bond and Barton MacLane as the very pictures of the stereotyped "flatfoot."

But it is Bogart's portrayal of Sam Spade that remains classic in its construction. Obviously cynical, he still maintains his own code of ethics which he adheres to faithfully. (No matter how much he may love Astor, he will not let her get away with murdering his partner.) He is brash, but not foolhardy. He is courageous, but not without fear. (An excellent scene finds him standing up to Greenstreet and telling him off while the Fat

THE MALTESE FALCON (1941). With director John Huston's father, Walter Huston, in an unbilled cameo appearance

Man's stooges stand by with guns. He then walks out of the hotel room slamming the door angrily and as he walks down the hallway we see him break into a broad smile, but he looks down at his hand and it is trembling. His bluff has worked, but it might have failed.) Where people, and especially women, are concerned he demands loyalty and truth. He can spot sham immediately. (He listens to Astor's long story with a straight face and then smiles, telling her, "You're good. You're *very* good," letting her know he sees right through her.)

This is the film role which molded the image we remember of Bogart all through the early years of the forties (an image elaborated upon and reinforced in *Casablanca*) and the one which all Bogart fans remember with great affection and admiration.

Bogart's first film of 1942, *All Through the Night,* is one of his less appreciated efforts of the early forties. Stylishly directed by Vincent Sherman, the film adroitly blended comedy and fast-paced action with the mystery and intrigue of wartime spy melodrama. Bogart was in good form as a wise-cracking Runyon-esque tough guy called "Gloves" Donahue, who set out to find the murderer of a friendly baker and soon found himself em-broiled in a nest of Nazi spies headed by Conrad Veidt, Peter Lorre, and Judith Anderson. Several things seriously deterred the film's success. It was released very shortly after the bombing of Pearl Harbor, a bad time for portraying a quasi-realistic spy tale in a laughable manner. The film also suffered from an overt case of "cuteness" in its dialogue, with such lines as "There's more to this than meets the F. B. I." being uttered all too

THE MALTESE FALCON (1941). With Peter Lorre, Mary Astor, and Sydney Greenstreet

frequently by Bogart and his comic retinue which included Frank McHugh, William Demarest, Jackie Gleason, and Phil Silvers. Another weak point in the film was a completely unbelievable "cliffhanger" ending which found Veidt driving a speedboat loaded with explosives toward a battleship and being thrwarted at the last minute by Bogart, who sends the Nazi toward a pile of floating lumber in a blazing finale. In spite of these minor irritants, the film did give Bogart a chance to do some very creditable comedy work and on the whole it still entertains.

His next film, *The Big Shot* (1942), was a minor setback in his burgeoning career artistically. A throwback to the quickie prison potboilers of the thirties, this weak entry found the actor lying on his death bed recounting the

ALL THROUGH THE NIGHT (1942). With Kaaren Verne

THE BIG SHOT (1942). With Joseph Downing and Irene Manning

series of circumstances and soap-opera contrivances responsible for his ultimate downfall. All the stock gimmicks were there, including the double-crossing lawyer (Stanley Ridges), the elaborate prison break (with a partner undeservedly being killed and an innocent friend caught in the middle and facing "grave" charges), the loyal moll (Irene Manning), and a swiftly paced car chase which almost exactly mirrored the motorized highlight of *High Sierra*. Almost resignedly, in a listless performance director Lewis Seiler could not spark, Bogart seemed to express the futility of his situation; a frank admittal that he had been through the whole thing before and knew, as we knew, just how it would turn out.

Not only did *Across the Pacific* (1942) add some luster to Bo-

ACROSS THE PACIFIC (1942). Bogart as Rick Leland

gart's rising stature as an actor, it more than justified the promise shown by director John Huston after his success with *The Maltese Falcon.* From a screenplay by Richard Macaulay, Huston turned what might have been a routine wartime espionage caper into a film which Bosley Crowther in *The New York Times* stated was "like having a knife at your ribs for an hour and a half." *Across the Pacific* did have its share of excitement with Bogart, at the climax of the film, virtually wiping out a whole contingent of Japanese soldiers as well as a bomb-laden plane set to attack the Panama Canal. (Superior special effects were very much in evidence.) The movie enhanced its conventional melodrama with an entertaining parade of full-bodied

ACROSS THE PACIFIC (1942). With director John Huston

CASABLANCA (1943). With Dooley Wilson

CASABLANCA (1943). With Ingrid Bergman

character studies. Sydney Greenstreet was excellent as a jovial yet cunning Japanese sympathizer and Mary Astor played an ambiguous role with the same dexterity she had displayed in *The Maltese Falcon.* But it was Bogart, of course, who carried the story line here and it was a delight to watch his enigmatic character change from one of calculated indifference to that of relentless determination. Huston was called to war duty before he finished this film (Vincent Donahue completed it), thus stifling any prospects of future collaboration with Bogart until *The Treasure of the Sierra Madre* five years later.

Bogart's next effort, *Casablanca* (1943), has become a recognized screen classic and is considered by many to be *the* representative picture of the forties. A glossy, star-laden sentimental melodrama, it, like *The Maltese Falcon,* owes its success to a gallery of fine performances and to their almost miraculous interplay with each other. Directed with flawless skill by Michael Curtiz, the plot, in a screenplay by Julius J. and Philip G. Epstein and Howard Koch (based on the play *Everybody Comes to Rick's* by Murray Burnett and Joan Alison), revolves about an assortment of strongly delineated characters coming into Rick's Café Américain, a night club and focal point for intrigue in Casablanca as refugees from Nazi-occupied Europe seek to gain exit visas to Lisbon.

Bogart, playing the café's owner, Rick, is a former soldier of fortune who has grown tired of smuggling and fighting and is now content to sit out the war in his own neutral territory. Even loyalty to a friend doesn't move him as he refuses to help Ugarte (Peter Lorre), a desperately frightened little courier who is fleeing from the police. (Ugarte is shot and killed only moments later, but not before he has given Rick two letters of transit.) Emphatically, Bogart says, "I stick my neck out for nobody." But we know he will do *just* that in a very short time, for into his quiet life comes a haunting vision from his past, the beautiful woman (Ingrid Bergman) he still loves and bitterly remembers. She is married to an underground leader (Paul Henreid) and she desperately needs those papers Bogart conveniently now has in his possession. The cynical Bogart's facade of neutrality begins to weaken as he recalls the bittersweet memories of his past love affair (memories triggered repeatedly when the strains of "As Time Goes By"

CASABLANCA (1943). With Paul Henreid, Ingrid Bergman, and Claude Rains.

come from Sam, his piano-playing confidante, played by Dooley Wilson). Bogart refuses to help her, still resentful of her desertion of him on the eve of their departure from Paris. She explains that she was married to Henreid at the time she fell in love with Bogart, believing him to have been killed, but when she found that her husband was alive she felt obligated to return to him. Bogart is convinced she is telling the truth and finally sets up an involved plan which succeeds when Bergman and Henreid are safely placed on the plane to Lisbon.

Intermixed in this intrigue are all the fascinating and beautifully acted supporting roles. With his customary skill, Claude Rains played Major Renault, a prefect of police who is like Bogart in many ways. He, too, claims neutrality, but is definitely against the Nazis. He is Bogart's most devoted adversary, tauntingly calling the man a "sentimentalist" and delivering his share of cynically amusing lines (When he makes a small bet and is encouraged to make a bigger one, he remarks that he is only a "*poor* corrupt official.") Rains shares the final memorable scene of the film as, after Bergman's plane takes off, he and Bogart walk off into the

misty night, two men who are both sentimentalists and now share the common bond of being patriots. As Major Strasser, Conrad Veidt was the very essence of German rigidity, unfeeling, unconcerned about life, but firmly believing in the foolish ideology of his Nazi compatriots. Sydney Greenstreet was Señor Farrari, a black marketeer on good terms with Bogart.

The magic that developed from the teaming of Bogart and Bergman was enough to make a new romantic figure out of the former tough guy. To his cynicism, his own code of ethics, his hatred of the phoniness in all human behavior, he now added the softening traits of tenderness and compassion and a feeling of heroic commitment to a cause. They helped him perfect the portrayal of the ideal man who all men wished to emulate.

One can look at hundreds of films produced during this period without finding any whose composite pieces fall so perfectly into place. Its photography by Arthur Edeson was outstanding, capturing the feeling of intrigue and intertwined lives with a vividness which made the viewer completely forget he was looking at a studio-built facsimile. The music score by Max Steiner was inventive,

ACTION IN THE NORTH ATLANTIC (1943). With Kane Richmond and Raymond Massey

ACTION IN THE NORTH ATLANTIC (1943). With Sam Levene, Alan Hale, and Raymond Massey

yet unobtrusive, and the editing by Owen Marks was concise and timed perfectly. Bogart's and Bergman's love scenes created a genuinely romantic aura, capturing a sensitivity between the two players one would not have believed possible. Even the release of the picture was perfectly timed, coming at the climax of an important Anglo-American conference in Casablanca.

Casablanca brought Bogart his first Academy Award nomination (he lost to Paul Lukas for *Watch On the Rhine*) and won Awards for Best Picture of the Year, Best Screenplay, and Best Director. (Not bad for a picture whose participants claimed they couldn't understand the plot even while they were making it.)

Bogart's second film of the year, *Action in the North Atlantic* (1943), started out as a two-reel tribute to the merchant marine, but was quickly expanded by Warner Brothers into a full-length action film. It contained all the stock clichés, including the well-integrated crew with each member delivering his own stereotyped ethnic exhortations, the traditional burial at sea of a prized compatriot, and much fist-shaking determination and invective hurtled at the enemy. All the performers took a back seat to the special effects and stunt departments as two spectacularly staged shipboard explosions and fires dominated the film. These incendiary holocausts seemed to literally engulf entire sound stages and the film's stars, Bogart and Raymond Massey, kiddingly made bets with each other as to whose stunt double was the braver. Miniature shots of entire ship convoys and enemy submarines were also far superior to the usual bathtub toys evident in so many similar efforts.

As, respectively, the lieutenant and captain aboard a merchant-marine ship, Bogart and Massey had little real chance to show much more than pure determination in their roles, but both alternated effectively between moments of tenderness when on shore with their loved ones (Julie Bishop for Bogart, Ruth Gordon for Massey) and rugged heroism on board ship. Both men uttered the usual wartime banalities as the enemy, consistently portrayed as vicious and inhuman, went about its business of machine-gunning men in lifeboats, maniacally smiling all the while. Crisply directed by Lloyd Bacon, *Action in the North Atlantic* remains one of the better examples of its genre.

SAHARA (1943). With Bruce Bennett

SAHARA (1943). Bogart as Sergeant Joe Gunn.

It appeared almost obligatory on the part of all the major film studios during World War II to present one or more all-star revues featuring as many of the lot's contract players as schedules would permit. Warner Brothers' first extravaganza, *Thank Your Lucky Stars* (1943; its second was the dreadful *Hollywood Canteen* a year later), gave extended bits to stars like Bette Davis (who sang), Errol Flynn (who danced), John Garfield (who did a radio sketch), and many others. All that was allotted to Bogart was an unmemorable, and unfunny, backstage bit where he is upbraided briefly by S. Z. ("Cuddles") Sakall and told to get out of the theater.

One cinema gambit that seldom fails to be a crowd pleaser is that of isolating a diverse collection of persons in a seemingly inescapable position and then decimating the group, either internally or externally, one by one. *The Lost Patrol* (1934), *Bataan* (1943), and *And Then There Were None* (1945) are just a few examples, and Columbia contributed to the category with *Sahara* (1943), a first-rate war film, well directed by Zoltan Korda, which qualitatively balanced its superb action sequences with penetrating char-

acter studies. Bogart, in his first non-Warner Brothers' film since *Stand-In,* was a tank commander who, when separated from his unit in the Libyan Desert, picks up a group of allied (and eventually several enemy) stragglers and heads out in search of badly needed water. Once they arrive at a nearly dry oasis, and after he learns that a motorized battalion of Germans is also after the water, Bogart decides to make a valiant stand. Predictably, almost all the group is wiped out and just when it appears that Bogart is about to be killed, his attackers give up, accepting defeat in return for water. Though propagandistic and overly idealistic in the style of most war-action films, Bogart's characterization was excellent as he gave what many considered to be the most realistic portrait of the truly "American" fighting man yet pictured on the screen. Assisting in the overall success of *Sahara* was a masterful musical score by Miklos Rozsa, who did similar duty the same year in another "tank" picture, Paramount's *Five Graves to Cairo.*

Wartime heroics never seemed exploited in quite so complex a fashion as in Bogart's only film of 1944, *Passage to Marseille,* directed by Michael Curtiz.

PASSAGE TO MARSEILLE (1944). A rare shot with director Michael Curtiz, Peter Lorre, and producer Hal Wallis

PASSAGE TO MARSEILLE (1944). With Peter Lorre, Helmut Dantine, and George Tobias

Bogart, a French journalist framed for murder because of his political views and sent to Devil's Island during World War II, escapes from his penal hell with four other convicts and winds up on a French freighter bound for home. Hoping to rejoin the fighting Free French resistance movement, the men, all fiercely loyal patriots, become involved in preventing a takeover of the ship by Fascist sympathizers. This relatively simple plot line was then surrounded by a series of extraneous plots and subplots which were related in a series of single, double, and even *triple* flashbacks, making any semblance of coherency virtually impossible. Bogart's characterization was equally vague and complicated as he maintained an opposing balance of virtue and vice. At one moment he is the picture of idealistic moral righteousness fighting against a callous system, and the next he is himself animalistic as he brutally machine-guns some defenseless enemies. His moral platitudes do not balance his immoral behavior, making for ambiguity and confusion. The most important saving grace of *Passage to Marseille* was the supporting cast headed by Bogart's *Casablanca* co-stars Claude Rains, Sydney Green-

street, and Peter Lorre, who all turned in strong character portrayals.

Warner Brothers was obviously trying to recreate the atmosphere and commercial success of *Casablanca* in Bogart's next film, *To Have and Have Not* (1945), but the results were only moderately successful and satisfying. The film was supposedly based on Ernest Hemingway's story, but scriptwriters Jules Furthman and William Faulkner used little from that source as they told the story of a skipper (Bogart) of a small fishing boat who is hired to smuggle a French underground leader and his wife into Martinique. (He agrees reluctantly, because he needs the money.) Adding excitement was a subplot which introduced Lauren Bacall to the screen as a stranded American with whom Bogart carries on an innocent flirtation which later develops into a more serious affair. Audience acceptance of the Bogart-Bacall team was instantaneous as the two became the screen's most talked-about new combination. Bacall's famous line to Bogart after she leaves his hotel room, "If you want me, just whistle. You know how to whistle, don't you? You just put your lips together—and blow," were etched in filmgoers' minds for

TO HAVE AND HAVE NOT (1945). With Lauren Bacall, Walter Brennan, and Hoagy Carmichael

TO HAVE AND HAVE NOT (1945). With Lauren Bacall and Dan Seymour

TO HAVE AND HAVE NOT (1945). With Lauren Bacall

years. The romance not only blossomed onscreen but off-screen as well as Bogart began to court the woman who would shortly become his fourth wife and make him a happy man for the remainder of his life.

Director Howard Hawks guided Bogart through a performance that was not far afield, though in no way as firmly delineated, from that of Rick in *Casablanca,* and Walter Brennan gave another strong performance as Bogart's booze-soaked pal. Those traits we now expected to see in Bogart were all there: his initially flippant attitude toward Bacall, whom he could love yet cast away, his loyalty to Brennan no matter what

the circumstances, his own brand of justice meted out to transgressors who do not play the game according to *his* set of rules and *his* code of ethics, and his perpetual concern for the underdog (in this case the underground leader and his wife) who seems to always embroil him in a perilous situation. *To Have and Have Not* was an excellent example of performers triumphing over their material. The film was remade as *The Breaking Point* (1951) with John Garfield and *The Gun Runners* (1958) with Audie Murphy and both were inferior to the original.

Confusion reigned in Bogart's next film. *Conflict* (1945) was an atmospheric piece of cinema hokum built around the much-overused gimmick of showing us how and by whom a murder is committed and then suffering us to wait for the fatal slip that will betray the perpetrator. Bogart was the scheming wife-killer and Sydney Greenstreet the rotund psychologist who drives him into confessing his guilt by setting enough visual traps to make Bogart believe that his wife is really still alive. Greenstreet and Alexis Smith, playing the murdered woman's younger sister, stole all the acting honors this time around as Bogart began to venture into new fields of characterization, deserting the image he had spent several years in cultivating in order to expand his scope as an actor. It was a foolishly unrewarding first attempt.

Having done justice earlier to Dashiell Hammett's Sam Spade in *The Maltese Falcon,* it was only a matter of time until Warner Brothers got around to another top-flight private eye in the person of Raymond Chandler's Philip Marlowe. (The character was to receive more than a fair share of screen exposure as he was portrayed by Dick Powell in *Murder, My Sweet* [1945], Robert Montgomery in *Lady in the Lake* [1946], George Montgomery in *The Brasher Dou-*

bloon [1947], and James Garner in *Marlowe* [1969]). Warners' vehicle was *The Big Sleep* (1946), an incredibly complex detective thriller that absolutely defies comprehension in a single screening. Even the film's stars complained that *they* didn't know what the whole thing was about, either. Bogart, now taking film assignments like this in stride, was hired ostensibly to track down a blackmailer, but quickly found himself immersed in murder, assorted double-crosses, and wanton mayhem. Even though one could hardly understand what was happening, Howard Hawks' expert direction and a well-chosen cast combined to keep the viewer enthralled with the film's peripheral virtues: dialogue, by William Faulkner and Leigh Brackett, that was concise and crackled with excitement; memorable scenes such as the one in which Bogart witnesses Bob Steele smilingly giving Elisha Cook, Jr., a poisoned glass of water, all the while assuring him that he has nothing to fear; and Bogart's coldly calculated shoot-out with Steele later in the film. Most filmgoers will also recall Bogart's entering the case and receiving his instructions in a humid, suffocating hothouse; the subtle humor and suggestive by-

CONFLICT (1945). With Alexis Smith

play of Bogart's quick flirtation with bookstore clerk Dorothy Malone; and all of Bogart's encounters with Lauren Bacall (who couldn't act very well, but who cared?) in her second leading role with the actor. If *The Big Sleep* was a somewhat flawed jewel, it nevertheless was an important contribution to the

Bogart mystique and is usually paired with *The Maltese Falcon* when reissued.

Bogart again ventured from his home base at Warner Brothers to do another picture for Columbia. *Dead Reckoning* (1947) was somewhat of a rehashing of the plots and dialogue of *The Maltese Falcon* and *The*

THE BIG SLEEP (1946). With Tom Fadden, John Ridgely, and Ben Weldon

Big Sleep, but it contained much more visual violence. Bogart was again portraying his now all-too-familiar role of the sardonic cynic with his own moral code who, this time, was on the trail of a killer who had murdered a wartime paratrooper buddy. Columbia cast Lizabeth Scott as Bogart's *femme fatale,* obviously hoping to exploit her close resemblance to Lauren Bacall. Unfortunately, like Bacall, her first few films found her equally awkward and expressionless. In one of the film's more sordid scenes, Bogart is beaten savagely by Marvin Miller, and later repays in kind by confronting Miller and Morris

Carnovsky and forcing them to divulge information by throwing fire bombs at them. The dialogue was typically hard-boiled and when Bogart finally exposes Scott's guilt and tells her "You're going to fry," it was an unmistakable echo of his line "You're going over for it," delivered to Mary Astor in a similar situation in *The Maltese Falcon*.

The Two Mrs. Carrolls (1947) was made in 1945, but its release was held up for almost two years. The reasons were quite apparent to most viewers who quickly decided, though Bogart had his own choice, that this was the actor's absolutely worst film in his career. Nothing has come along to refute that general consensus. Bogart was unbelievably cast as an American artist living in London who uses his first wife as a model for his painting, "The Angel of Death," and then dispatches her with a glass of poisoned milk. Enter Barbara Stanwyck, who falls into the same pattern as Bogart decides to paint an encore. Amid a plethora of complications, Stanwyck finally finds out what Bogart is up to and they have a bizarre confrontation in which both stars try to outdo each other in overacting. Bogart seemed fretfully amateurish as he mugged his way through this dreary business.

DEAD RECKONING (1947). With Morris Carnovsky and Marvin Miller

THE TWO MRS. CARROLLS (1947). With Barbara Stanwyck

Bogart's third teaming with Lauren Bacall was in *Dark Passage* (1947), a murder-mystery film which depended upon contrivances rather than good scripting to see it through. The film opened with the use of a subjective camera (MGM used it throughout their *Lady in the Lake* that same year) with Bogart's off-camera narration establishing the plot as we watch our hero escape from prison with the intent of finding the real murderer of his wife, the crime for which he had been wrongfully jailed. Once he meets up with Bacall and goes to a plastic surgeon, the subjective camera is forgotten as Bogart now utilizes his own face and carries on the investigation. *Dark Passage* was energetically directed and written by Delmer Daves who used some atmospheric location shots in San Francisco to underscore his drama. The film included an unusual number of bizarre and eccentric characters, all competently played. Agnes Moorehead, who turns out to be the real killer, essayed a superbly schizoid characterization as a bitchy "friend" of Bogart and his dead wife. Bacall showed definite signs of improvement in her acting and Bogart was properly acerbic and nonplussed, even when Moorehead, his alibi, falls to her death from an apartment window. He simply takes off for South America to start a new life with Bacall.

For all practical purposes, this film marked the conclusion of Bogart's famous "image" period. Now he was to forsake his romantic leading-man roles for acting assignments which he hoped would raise him to greater heights as a performer. He was to succeed, in many cases, magnificently.

DARK PASSAGE (1947). With Lauren Bacall

Having had his day as an idolized star and romantic leading man, it was now time for Bogart to get down to the serious business of acting. For eighteen years it had usually been Bogart playing Bogart in various shadings. Now *that* Bogart was gone and in his place was an older and far less romantic figure, one who found new challenges and was able to meet most of them successfully. This new phase of his continued growth began with a story of three men in search of gold.

Although *The Treasure of the Sierra Madre* (1948) is indisputably one of Bogart's best films, it was co-star Walter Huston who won an Academy Award as did the movie's director and scenarist, John Huston. Based on a novel by the mysterious B. Traven, the film told a riveting tale which explored the degenerative effects of encroaching greed, distrust, and hatred on three down-on-their-luck wastrels who team up to search for gold in Mexico. Bogart's Fred C. Dobbs was an amazingly complex creation whose slow disintegration into paranoia was brilliantly managed on camera. He is a born loser with no potential for change in sight. Suspicious, unfeeling, savage, and easily corruptible, he seems clearly des-

THE TREASURE
AND
THE QUEEN

tined for a tragic fate almost from our first meeting with him. Tim Holt, in a role originally announced for John Garfield, was also excellent as Curtin, a man who, like Bogart, is tempted but whose conscience will not permit him to exercise his baser desires. (He could have let Bogart die in a cave-in, but saved him instead.) Young, impressionable, and unprepared, he has never seen the likes of a Fred C. Dobbs and he finds himself overwhelmed and uncertain as to how he will cope with Dobbs's rage and greed. However, it is the director's father, Walter Huston, who literally stole the picture from both Bogart and Holt as he played Howard, a wise old toothless codger who knew all along what would happen and took it all in stride, kicking up his heels and having a marvelous time. Life can't surprise him any more. He's already had successes and failures enough for one lifetime. Like a faithful dog, he's along for the thrill of the hunt, and should there be another pot of gold at the end of this rainbow, well,

THE TREASURE OF THE SIERRA MADRE (1948). With Tim Holt

THE TREASURE OF THE SIERRA MADRE (1948). With Tim Holt

that's just a bonus.

It is mainly the interreaction of these three men from their first meeting and uneasy partnership through their final confrontation that made *The Treasure of the Sierra Madre* one of Warner Brothers' triumphs of the forties. The studio had actually bought the original story before World War II and had attempted treatments several times. Fortunately, they waited until Huston had returned from his war duty so that he could handle the job he really had wanted to do for many years. It was producer Henry Blanke, whom Huston was to acknowledge when he received his "Oscar," who talked Jack Warner into letting Huston go to Mexico for two expensive months of location shooting. As the daily rushes were screened, Warner became increasingly concerned about this offbeat film. He didn't want Bogart to be killed at the end, but lost that argument under Huston and Blanke's continued pressure. Despite all the difficulties, the result was a film and a Bogart performance whose luster seems to brighten with every screening.

Obviously anxious to work again with Huston, Bogart immediately started filming *Key Largo* (1948). For Bogart *Key Largo* was another *The Petrified Forest,* but this time *he* was the disenchanted idealist and Edward G. Robinson the vicious, antiquated symbol of raw brute force. Paul Muni had appeared in the original Maxwell Anderson play in 1939, and director John Huston and Richard Brooks updated the piece to make it more contemporary. As a film, it was treated in a slightly heavy-handed, overly talky manner, displacing action in favor of strong character studies of a group of disparate individuals trapped by kingpin gangster Johnny Rocco (Robinson) in an isolated hotel on a Florida key. Claire Trevor won an Academy Award as Gaye Dawn, Rocco's boozy mistress who was willing to lower herself to any depths for the mere expedient of getting a drink. She is finally pushed too far by Rocco, has accepted too many insults and been rejected once too often, and she decides to help the beleaguered prisoners. Lauren Bacall was Nora Temple, an antiseptic dreamer who persisted in believing that evil should always be opposed by a valiant Sir Galahad and temporarily has her illusions shattered when Bogart apparently doesn't agree to fit into her mold. As Bacall's grandfather,

KEY LARGO (1948). As Frank McCloud, an ex-army major who finds himself in peril

KEY LARGO (1948). With Claire Trevor and Edward G. Robinson

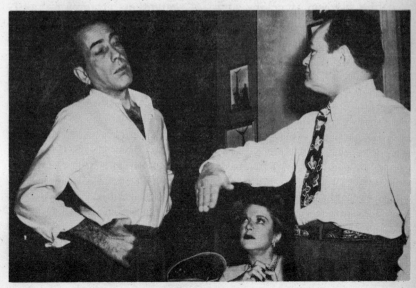

Lionel Barrymore was another heroic figure who could afford to be a verbal hero, knowing that a retreat to the safety of his confining wheelchair could protect him.

Edward G. Robinson as Rocco was a mass of contradictions. Brutal with a gun safely in his hand, dreaming of the glories he once knew in the good old days when he was a big shot, all he has left are the memories. He is a man whose criminal wisdom permits no ethics (he offers Bogart an empty gun to shoot it out with him) and few feelings. He is also a man afraid, who sweats when the hurricane approaches and poses a threat to his safety. He abhors Bogart because of his wartime heroism, mocking and taunting him because his courage is something alien in Rocco's own unheroic life. As war hero Frank McCloud, Bogart was the most complex character of all. Disillusioned, tired of his war-induced killings, unwilling to risk himself in any new test of courage ("One Rocco more or less isn't worth dying for"), he is now a complacent shadow of his former noble self. He, like Barrymore, seeks an idyllic world where "there's no place for Johnny Roccos." However, his pattern has been too well established. He, like Claire Trevor, can be pushed only so far and then reason and restraint seem no longer acceptable as an alternative to action. In a violent showdown, he succeeds in killing Rocco. It is these people who breathe life into the film, and though *Key Largo* may lack substance and coherence it is first-rate drama and entertainment.

In 1947, Bogart had formed his own producing company, Santana Productions, and signed to appear in four films to be released through Columbia Pictures. The first of these, *Knock On Any Door* (1949), was a major disappointment. With a screenplay by Daniel Taradash and John Monks, Jr., and directed by Nicholas Ray, the film was a pretentious attempt to glorify a young hoodlum (John Derek). Bogart played a forceful attorney who spent almost the entire film trying to convince the jury and the audience that Derek was an innocent victim of circumstantial evidence. To prove his point, he took the audience through a series of flashbacks into the sordid squalor and deprivation that brought about the killing in question. Finally, just when everyone is about convinced, the district attorney tears into Derek, who falls apart and confesses his guilt. Bogart, having truly believed him in-

KNOCK ON ANY DOOR (1949). With George Macready, Barry Kelley, and John Derek

nocent, then delivers an unconvincing diatribe which ends with him shaking his finger at the jury and the camera and announcing: "Knock on any door and you may find a Nick Romano." The film was a patently phony attempt at social commentary which simply didn't come off. A sequel, *Let No Man Write My Epitaph,* was made in 1960. One line of dialogue from *Knock On Any Door,* used as Derek's motto, was often quoted by young people in the fifties: "Live fast, die young, and make a good-looking corpse."

Tokyo Joe (1949), the second film in Bogart's Columbia deal, was very likely the worst of the four Santana offerings. Bogart was a flyer who returned after World War II to Tokyo to pick up his life with a wife (Florence Marly) he had deserted, only to find that she had remarried and was the mother of his seven-year-old daughter. In the ensuing complications, Bogart is placed in a position where he must smuggle some Japanese war criminals back into Japan or his daughter will be killed. In an example of foolhardy heroics, Bogart sacrifices his life to save that of the young girl. It was all tritely concocted derring-do and Bogart was much less convincing than in his *Across the Pacific* days, where he was also required to deal with villainous Japanese. For an actor who had belabored the point that he had been forced to do too many bad films because he had no control over the properties, it was disappointing to see him making extremely bad films now that he *did* have full control.

In 1950, jet planes were a relatively recent phenomenon and their emergence offered new possibilities for the long-defunct test-pilot genre of film. In *Chain Lightning* (1950), Bogart was a World War II bomber pilot hired as a test-pilot who, after the death of his designer friend (Richard Whorf), successfully tries out a newly designed ejection cockpit. However, there was little value in a film in which a line like "JA-3 to Fort George. I am fifty miles North of you—ooooops, I just passed you!" was fairly commonplace. Eleanor Parker offered the only creative acting in the role of Raymond Massey's secretary and Bogart's love interest. Unhappy with drivel like this, Bogart would soon terminate his contract with Warner Brothers.

Bogart was well accustomed to

TOKYO JOE (1949). With Florence Marly and Alexander Knox

CHAIN LIGHTNING (1950). With Eleanor Parker

criminally inspired violence, but in *In A Lonely Place* (1950), the third and best of his four Santana Productions for Columbia, he had to portray the personal inner turmoil of a psychopathic Hollywood writer given to savage, uncontrollable rages which nearly bring tragedy to everyone he comes in contact with. The irritatingly moody yet absorbing script by Andrew Solt was given deft direction by Nicholas Ray as it surrounded its cast of characters in a circle of murder, violence, and suspicion. Bogart gave one of his best latter-day portrayals as a principal suspect

in the murder of a hatcheck girl. At times loving and sensitive, Bogart was fearful to behold when his seemingly natural inclination toward violence took control. He was chillingly convincing as he beat a youth into senselessness after a minor auto accident, or almost strangled the girl he loved, who is the one person who could possibly help him become a rational human being. (Gloria Grahame played the girl with a brooding sensitivity in one of her best roles.) We were to see Bogart mentally disintegrate several times (*The Treasure of the Sierra Madre* and *The Caine*

Mutiny are the two best examples), but never so completely and with such stinging force.

Bogart regained his screen composure and returned to Warner Brothers to do a type of role he knew very well. *The Enforcer* (1951) offered Bogart nothing more than a composite portrait of roles he had mastered earlier in his career. He was a crusading assistant district attorney who was out to snare the head of Murder, Inc. (Everett Sloane). Bretaigne Windust's taut direction kept things moving at a rapid pace with an unusually generous helping of rapid-fire dialogue supplied by writer Martin Rackin, but the plot seemed unnecessarily complicated. Particularly graphic scenes of violence included gangster Ted De Corsia falling to his death in a futile escape attempt, and the dredging up of a gangland graveyard. This was to be Bogart's final film for Warner Brothers, the end of a relationship marked by years of unfulfillment that finally evolved into years of personal success and superior screen achievement.

Now free of contract obligations elsewhere, Bogart wrapped

IN A LONELY PLACE (1950). With Frank Lovejoy, Jeff Donnell, and Gloria Grahame

THE ENFORCER (1951). With Roy Roberts and Zero Mostel

up his commitment to Columbia. Few of Bogart's many film characterizations were as unsavory as that of gunrunner Harry Smith, a role he essayed in the final entry in Santana Production's four-picture deal, *Sirocco* (1951). Bogart seemed destined for a painful end as he plied his despicable trade in a tale set in French-occupied Damascus around 1925. Casting his lot between the French and Syrians, depending upon which suits his own greedy plan most profitably, he earns the enmity of both sides. It is finally the Syrians who give Bogart his final reward by lobbing a hand grenade at him in the film's finale. There were good supporting performances by Lee J. Cobb, thumping his desk as usual as a French colonel, and Everett Sloane as a volatile general, but the film was of little consequence and a sorry end to Bogart's solo production credits. (He did co-produce *Beat the Devil* three years later, with more satisfying results.)

Very much needing a successful picture after six relatively unrewarding efforts, Bogart found an ideal showcase for his abilities in *The African Queen* (1952). *The African Queen* was Bogart's fourth film to be directed by John Huston and his performance in it was very likely the best in his career as well as one which finally won him an Academy Award. (He beat out Marlon Brando, who was heavily favored to win for *A Streetcar Named Desire.*) The screenplay by Huston and the celebrated movie critic-writer, James Agee, matched Bogart with Katherine Hepburn in what amounted to a two-star tour de force in a subtly conceived semi-spoof of wartime heroics. Bogart played Charlie Allnut, a gin-soaked skipper of a dilapidated river launch (called "The African Queen)," who is browbeaten and coerced by Rose Sayer (Hepburn), a prissy, puritanical pillar of virtue and determina-

tion, into taking them via his boat to attack a German gunboat. Their journey is plagued by the elements and their verbal sparring with each other, but ends when they succeed in their mission and in their ultimate understanding, acceptance, and affection for each other. Bogart and Hepburn were delightful as they infused their personal conflict with a warmth, humor (which was lacking in C. S. Forester's original story), and tenderness seldom seen in films. Bogart played many scenes with maximum effectiveness, including the grueling river trek where he becomes covered with leeches and suffers a severe fever attack, his drunk scene where he rebels against Hepburn and mocks her

SIROCCO (1951). With Lee J. Cobb

118

THE AFRICAN QUEEN (1951). With Katharine Hepburn

THE AFRICAN QUEEN (1951). Bogart, as the skipper of an antiquated riverboat, sets off to attack a German gunboat

THE AFRICAN QUEEN (1951). As Charlie Allnut, the role which won him an Academy Award

high-blown speeches, and the tender moments in which he realizes he's fallen under her bewitching spell.

The African Queen was not an easy film to make, most of it being done on location in the insect-infested, suffocatingly humid African Congo. Hepburn and others in the company became quite ill, causing some temporary delays. There were other tribulations. "The African Queen" really sank and it took three days to get it afloat again, and the camp was attacked by an army of safari ants, all making a difficult undertaking even more difficult. But the result was a brilliantly entertaining film, and *The African Queen* was one of 1952's top moneymakers. John Huston remarked to Bogart some time after the actor had won his Academy Award, "It's like I said, kid. Real leeches pay off in the long run!"

Bogart's performing capabilities reached their zenith in *The African Queen,* and now in the closing stages of his career he was to choose vehicles which appealed to him personally for one reason or another. Some of his choices were poor and his performances seemed regressive, bringing back memories of earlier failures, but others were quite substantial and in these he gave memorable interpretations. Even in his last film, when illness was beginning to take hold of him, he was still able to muster enough of his strength and talent to finish his screen career with a solid performance.

However, this period began with a film of relatively little value. Director Richard Brooks did a fairly creditable job with Bogart in *Deadline—U.S.A.* (1952), but the complexities of his own script marred the final result. Bogart was extremely hampered by a triple plot which found him battling to save a floundering newspaper from being sold, tangling with his ex-wife (Kim Hunter) and her new suitor, and crusading to uncover evidence against a murderous crime czar (Martin Gabel). The film was at its best when it was giving an absorbing semidocumentary treatment to the everyday problems of running a giant

THE FINAL YEARS

newspaper, but became sluggish when the overburdened plot slowed things down. Bogart played his role with vigor and was particularly appealing and sensitive in his scenes with Ethel Barrymore, who played the widow of the newspaper's founder.

Bogart immediately followed *Deadline—U.S.A.* with an appearance in *Battle Circus* (1953), another vehicle written and directed by Richard Brooks, with less satisfying results. Very likely the major fault was in teaming Bogart with June Allyson, an actress of extremely limited range whose perpetually simpering attitude and breathy whining of lines must surely have kept Bogart's nerves on edge. The idea of the film was a sound one, a semi-documentary approach at portraying the day-by-day activities of a mobile field hospital behind the front lines during the Korean War. The film fell apart, however, when an almost juvenile love plot interceded. One laughable scene found Allyson disarming a partially crazed prisoner who

DEADLINE—U.S.A. (1952). With Ed Begley, Joe De Santis, and Paul Stewart

was threatening to blow everyone up with a hand grenade, thereby proving her courage under fire to a rather uninterested Bogart, who finally falls in love with her.

"It stinks," was Bogart's initial reaction to the first-draft script of his next film, *Beat the Devil* (1954), written by John Huston, Anthony Veiller, and Peter Viertel. This was certainly a disappointing remark from the man who owned the screen rights to the original novel and who believed the story had the ingredients to become another *The Maltese Falcon*. Obviously director John Huston concurred and he brought Truman Capote

from the United States to the remote town of Ravello, Italy, where the bulk of photography on the film was completed, to do a complete rewrite. What had originally been envisioned as a relatively straight drama soon gave way to satire in its wildest possible form. The result was virtually unintelligible. A celebrated quote from Harry Kurnitz, the noted playwright, seemed appropriate: "No matter where you come in during its running, you seem to have missed at least half the picture." Bogart did have enough faith in the project, however, to invest more than a half-million dollars of his own money and act as an

122

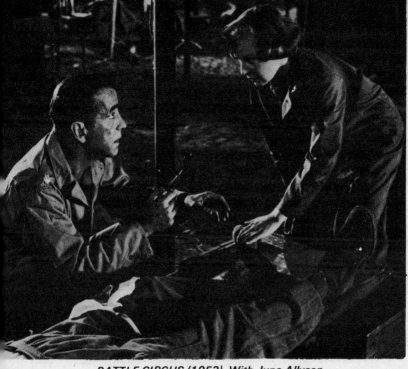

BATTLE CIRCUS (1953). With June Allyson

unbilled producer.

The plot, if you can call it that, concerned a group of six stranded adventurers in an Italian port whose plan is to buy up some East African land that supposedly contains uranium. Double-crossing quickly becomes the name of the game as Bogart and his fellow conspirators (including Robert Morley, Peter Lorre, Gina Lollobrigida, and a seemingly endless parade of bizarre characters) outdo each other in inspired zaniness.

Bogart, trying desperately to maintain his composure, delivered such priceless lines as: "I'm only in on this because the doctor told me I needed plenty of money. Without money I become dull, listless, and have trouble with my complexion." But his lines weren't the only offbeat ones. In a room where he is being questioned after being captured, while a firing squad goes about its routine work outside, he is asked straight-faced, "Now tell me, do you really know Rita Hayworth?"

The film is one of those rare

BEAT THE DEVIL (1954). With Gina Lollobrigida

BEAT THE DEVIL (1954). With Robert Morley

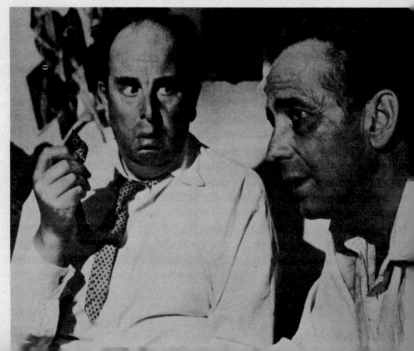

items that viewers either seem to love or hate, no middle ground accepted. Bogart himself called it a "mess" and declared that only the "phonies" thought it was really funny. Many reviewers thought the whole thing was a tasteless joke and decried the waste of time, talent, and money. Still others considered it one of the best screen satires ever made. *The New York Times* shared the latter view, but stated that "the fun wears mighty thin". In any case, Bogart gave an immensely satisfying performance in his tongue-in-cheek role and the film itself has now become a regular attraction in Bogart film retrospectives. It is also an excellent example of how much Bogart had matured as an actor, since it is not easy to overcome apparently inept material and still give a performance with some meaning and substance.

Bogart returned from his comedic European venture to a project with considerably more merit. The actor was producer Stanley Kramer's instant choice to play Captain Queeg when he obtained the screen rights to Herman Wouk's sprawling sea novel, *The Caine Mutiny*. Bogart remained his choice, in spite of pressure from those who said he was too old and that Richard Widmark would be bet-

ter, through the fifteen long months it took to get the film underway. (The navy refused to give its cooperation because the story dealt with a navy mutiny.) The decision was justified when director Edward Dmytryk guided Bogart through a memorable performance and one which earned him his third Academy Award nomination. (He lost to Marlon Brando in *On the Waterfront.*) A story of bravery and cowardice at odds with one another, *The Caine Mutiny* (1954) allowed Bogart to further expand his previous pattern of psychopathic disintegration he had shown in *The Treasure of the Sierra Madre,* the main difference here being that there was no motive of greed to trigger the change in Queeg's character. Queeg was simply a man who had seen too much of war. Decidedly loyal and undoubtably valiant in former times, he couldn't take the strain of command any longer and he fell easy prey to the machinations of self-serving officers who envied his position of leadership.

One of the major flaws of *The Caine Mutiny* is that it tried to tell too much within its restricted running time. A silly subplot between two young lovers (Robert Francis and May Wynn) only served to dilute and divert our

THE CAINE MUTINY (1954). With E. G. Marshall and Robert Bray (right)

attention from the real story. Also, the entire finale, an extended trial sequence, was clearly anticlimactic, though it contained the film's most taut and memorable scene, that of Queeg disintegrating as he delivered his testimony. But we had seen it all before, after all, aboard the ship. We had seen Queeg come apart at the seams, so we *knew* what would happen when he got on the stand, making the whole sequence rather superfluous. Bogart always claimed that he didn't like the part of Queeg because he didn't understand it and wasn't sure how to play it. Some critics agreed, claiming it

was one of Bogart's poorest performances, but most felt it was one of the actor's more interesting and satisfying characterizations.

Bogart's well-cultivated penchant for making enemies was never more evident than during the making of his next film, *Sabrina* (1954). Originally, director Billy Wilder had hoped to obtain Cary Grant for his leading man, and the script of the film was specifically tailored for him. When Grant pulled out at the last minute, Wilder had to settle for the only acceptable actor currently available, Humphrey Bogart. Wilder was forced to do a major rewrite to accommodate his new star. Almost immediately Bogart began to antagonize co-star William Holden, claiming that Holden "mugged" in scenes and that he was at best a mediocre actor. When Holden heard about the remarks he threatened to kill Bogart and had to be physically restrained by Wilder from carrying out his threat. Thereafter, and to this day, Holden never missed an opportunity to verbally attack Bogart in the press. Even petite Audrey Hepburn, *Sabrina*'s leading lady, was the target of Bogart's darts: "She's all right, if you don't mind a dozen takes." (Of course, her remark that Bogart was extremely nervous during their romantic scenes may have primed him.) Even Wilder, who could be as crude, or even cruder depending upon the circumstances, could not hit it off with Bogart.

In spite of the off-camera shenanigans, *Sabrina* was generally regarded as a successful comedy-romance. Adapted by Wilder, Samuel Taylor, and Ernest Lehman from Taylor's play, *Sabrina Fair,* the story was basically a Cinderella tale. Hepburn was a chauffeur's daughter who had aspirations to marry her wealthy employer's son (Holden). When he spurns her, she attempts suicide but is saved and sent off to Paris to become a cultivated lady, and on her return Holden has second thoughts. Enter Bogart as the older brother, intending to break up the courtship by pretending to fall in love with her himself. Naturally, as all good fairy tales must end, Bogart happily winds up as Hepburn's choice.

For an actor who had few opportunities to play comedy, Bogart's performance was surprisingly adroit. He somehow managed to temper conventional aristocratic stuffiness with incisive wit and charm. A challenge few actors could readily meet.

The Barefoot Contessa (1954), Bogart's fourth film made during a very active and successful year, opens at the rain-drenched gravesite of actress Maria Vargas (Ava Gardner) where the people who were involved with her recount how she arrived at this grim destination. They include Bogart as a film director and Edmond O'Brien, who won an Academy Award for his performance as a loud-mouthed press agent. Bogart relates how, as a director on the skids, he was hired to write a screenplay featuring a new glamor girl. He and a coarse millionaire interested in movie-making (Warren Stevens)

SABRINA (1954). With William Holden and Walter Hampden.

SABRINA (1954). A publicity shot which seems to capture Bogart's real feelings toward co-star Audrey Hepburn

THE BAREFOOT CONTESSA (1954). With Ava Gardner

discover Maria dancing in a Madrid cabaret and choose her as their leading lady. She becomes an overnight sensation and helps Bogart regain his lost stature. The remainder of this overlong film then turns to pretentious soap-opera, building to a climax in which Maria and a boyfriend are shot to death by her impotent husband (Rossano Brazzi). The film was populated by bitter, self-indulgent, and unsavory men who all came off second-best to Bogart, a cynical but comparatively likable character. The plot had strong cinematic possibilities, but the script by Joseph L. Mankiewicz, who also directed, had too many florid and ambiguous passages and ultimately became tiresome.

At this particular juncture in Bogart's life when he had managed to mature as a dramatic actor, it is difficult to understand why he chose to star next in a gentle comedy that demanded subtle abilities he simply did not possess. Although Bogart himself expressed a certain fondness for his newest venture, *We're No Angels* (1955), the film was not a very satisfactory showcase for his talent. Indeed, it was his weakest effort since *The Two Mrs. Carrolls.*

On the Broadway stage, where it was titled *My Three Angels* (adapted from the French play, *La Cuisine des Anges*), the vehicle was a charming, delicate little gem which told the story of three convicts who escape from Devil's Island on Christmas Eve and happen upon a family which is being besieged by an avaricious relative anxious to run them out of their small dry-goods store. The three escapees, who had originally planned to rob and murder the family, mellow ("Cutting their throats might spoil their Christmas") and decide to become the beleaguered family's guardian angels by first helping them put their business back on a paying basis, and then by eliminating their human predator by means of a poisonous pet viper.

On the stage Walter Slezak in the leading role gave an ebullient performance under Jose Ferrer's direction, and *My Three Angels* was enthusiastically received by most playgoers. However, when the play was transferred to the screen all subtleties seemed to disappear in a morass of gaudy overproduction and insensitive direction by Michael Curtiz. Lines which flowed from Slezak's mouth with seeming honesty and gentleness came out of Bogart with a bite and falseness which betrayed the author's intent. Aldo Ray and Peter Us-

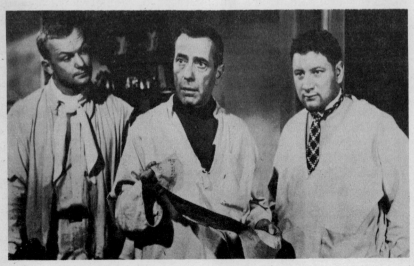

WE'RE NO ANGELS (1955). With Aldo Ray and Peter Ustinov

tinov were of little assistance as the other convicts and the whole film became an overly talkative bore. *My Three Angels* was simply too fragile a creature to be transferred to the giant screen and we must fault Bogart for not having the good judgment to pass it by in favor of something he could more adequately handle.

Even as late as 1955, Twentieth Century-Fox was still playing with its new visual toy, CinemaScope, and a long string of essentially bland stories surrounded by beautifully photographed scenic landscapes kept pouring from the studio's production centers. *The Left Hand of God* (1955), directed by Edward Dmytryk, was one of these barren efforts and Bogart was the victim of an inconsequential script by Alfred Hayes that found him portraying an American flyer forced down in China during World War II who joins up with a Chinese war lord (Lee J. Cobb, completely miscast in what writer Richard Gehman described as "one of the great unintentionally funny portrayals of all time"). When Bogart decides to escape, he assumes the garb of a murdered priest and finds seclusion in a remote mission. The role had great potential for suspense as

Bogart had to face one crisis after another as a result of his masquerade, but for some reason his performance was overly restrained and unrewarding.

For fifteen years (since *High Sierra*), Bogart had assiduously avoided playing his old familiar role as "the guy with the gat". Portraying despicable hoods and getting rubbed out at the end simply didn't appeal to him any more. The huge commercial success of Joseph Hayes' Broadway hit, *The Desperate Hours*, apparently rekindled his interest, though, and he agreed to play onscreen the role created on stage by Paul Newman.

In hideous contrast to the three lovable, but murderous, convicts of *We're No Angels, The Desperate Hours* (1955) gave us a triumvirate of the most ruthless and unsavory gangsters the screen has yet seen in what happily turned out to be a sizzling melodrama. The escaped convicts use guns to force their way into a quiet suburban household headed by Fredric March and Martha Scott. While there, Bogart, aided by his brother (Dewey Martin) and another partner (Robert Middleton), manages to heap indignity after indignity on the hapless captives. The audience is treated to an unrelenting portrait of

THE LEFT HAND OF GOD (1955). As Jim Carmody

brute force as Bogart unleashes his verbal and physical venom in a devastating portrayal of a man with no human feeling—a savage animal without pity, without concern, without virtue. Once before, in *The Petrified Forest,* Bogart gave us such a man, but that performance was relatively restrained compared to this beast at bay.

Under William Wyler's taut direction, Bogart was exceptionally convincing in the role, but for some reason the film did not achieve the success it merited. There are two possible reasons why it failed to live up to its promise. First, Bogart's age may have been an influence. On the stage, the much younger Paul Newman could verbally and physically command a greater believability than the older Bogart. Harassed captives might entertain thoughts of tackling an over-the-hill Bogart—never a menacing Newman. The second fault lies in the writing itself. Bogart, after all his viciousness and victimization, allows Fredric March to actually leave his home and proceed to continue his workday schedule under threat of harming his wife and children if he does not return or follow appropriate instructions. The fact that March chooses to follow instructions is difficult to believe. As the picture of integrity and virtue, would he allow an animal like Bogart to have free rein with his life and his family without at least going to the police to form some plan? Were Bogart and his cohorts reasonable criminals with reasonable feelings and instincts, we might not question his failure to act. But under the circumstances, we must conjecture that it is a script weakness, and it only takes one such lapse in credibility to seriously curtail a picture's effectiveness. Aside from Bogart's personal unhappiness with the picture's commercial failure, his performance is one of his best.

Bogart also delivered a powerful performance in his final screen role. By 1956 the boxing film had greatly diminished in appeal. Exceptional entries in the category such as *Body and Soul* (1947), *Champion* (1949) and *The Set-Up* (1949), with their fierce concentration on men who seek fame in the ring regardless of personal cost, rapidly gave way to the banalities of such films as *Iron Man* (1951), *The Square Jungle* (1955) and *World In My Corner* (1956).

Suddenly, like a breath of clear, invigorating air, came *The Harder They Fall* (1956). Here was an uncompromising, brutally frank fight drama told in terms of the human viciousness of the game's promoters rather than in the stereotyped travail of the fighter himself. Bogart played an ex-sports columnist who readily enters into an unholy alliance with a crooked promoter (Rod Steiger) to push an imported Argentinian giant, possessing little real ability, into the championship through a series of fixed bouts. The screenplay, fashioned by Philip Yordan from a novel by Budd Schulberg, bristled with crisp, brittle, totally realistic dialogue, and Mark Robson's direction was assured. However, for all the film's virtues, including the very wise decision to film it in the harshness

THE DESPERATE HOURS (1955).
As Glenn Griffin

THE DESPERATE HOURS (1955). **With Fredric March**

THE HARDER THEY FALL (1956). With Nehemiah Persoff and Rod Steiger

of black and white at a time when most films were being made in color, the film does have some certainly debatable flaws. Initially, it fails as a strong Bogart film, for it is not Bogart's performance that is memorable. Rather, it is Rod Steiger's portrayal of a thoroughly despicable man that garners our attention. Another weakness is the unconvincing compromise at the film's close. Throughout the entire film, Bogart's characterization runs almost parallel to that of Steiger's in that he too is morally corruptible and generally contemptible. Therefore, at the end of the film, when Bogart becomes disgusted at Steiger's treatment of their fighter and decides not only to pay him out of his own tainted share but threatens to write a series of exposés of the fight racket, we must question the logic of this artificially introduced attempt to have a happy ending. These minor drawbacks reflect in no way, of course, on Bogart's interpretation, which was flawless.

Physically Bogart's yet undetected illness was already beginning to take its toll. His voice was huskier than usual (and rumor has it that noted voice impressionist Paul Frees actually had to redub some of the actor's lines) and his face was beginning to look extremely drawn and haggard onscreen. At the conclusion of this film, Bogart was signed to star in *The Good Shepherd,* a British naval story set in World War II. He was not to begin it, or any of many other contemplated projects, and *The Harder They Fall* remains as his final contribution to the screen.

It has been more than fifteen years since Bogart died, yet he seems to be more strongly entrenched as a popular screen hero today than during his own lifetime. Through countless television screenings of his old films, as well as innumerable showcasings of his screen classics in festivals around the world, a whole new generation of filmgoers seems to have found in Bogart a kindred cinematic spirit with which they can closely identify.

But why Bogart? Why not James Cagney, Gary Cooper, James Stewart, or one of a dozen other durable screen actors? What special characteristics did this man possess in his screen image that sets him apart from all of his contemporaries? Why does Woody Allen write a play (*Play It Again, Sam*) which expresses the dream that he, like so many others, has to be *like* Bogart? Why can the screening of a Bogart film classic like *Casablanca,* which has been run innumerable times before, still have enough drawing power to pull larger ratings for an independent New York television station than an important presidential nominating convention can muster on the major networks?

There are no easy answers to these questions, of course. The

THE LEGEND

screen character of Bogart is so complex in its conception that it defies easy analysis. Every individual seems to recognize in Bogart those qualities that *he* wants to see in the character. If you are a romantic, Bogart is your ideal lover, mixing toughness with tenderness opposite Ingrid Bergman in *Casablanca* or Lauren Bacall in *To Have and Have Not* or Ida Lupino in *High Sierra.* If you are fascinated by the criminal in action, you no doubt will applaud Bogart's seemingly endless parade of gangster portrayals from the thirties. If you are inclined toward heroics, is there any man you've ever seen who is more valiant than the Bogart of *Sahara, Across the Pacific,* and *Action in the North Atlantic*? The variety seems relatively endless. No matter what you seek, somewhere in one of those seventy-five-or-so films that Bogart made you will find just the sort of man you are looking for.

Perhaps we can gain better insight into Bogart's lasting charisma if we can examine how certain general groups of individuals tend to react to him.

It is young people who seem particularly susceptible to Bogart's somewhat Bohemian image. In an age where the iconoclast seems to be the rule rather than the exception, Bogart appears to stand as the revered founder of the breed. His off-screen battles with the pretentious side of society, his conflicts with studio heads and pompous Hollywood personalities on all levels during his lifetime, stir sympathetic feelings. Bogart expressed his liberal, sometimes even ultra-radical, views when it was unfashionable, and often dangerous from the viewpoint of job stability, to do so. When the government began its sordid witch hunts in the forties and fifties in the film industry, it was always Bogart who was a leader in opposing its tyranny. Bogart was fighting for equal rights for minorities long before it became *the* cause to champion. He spoke his mind in public and in private and held nothing back, regardless of whom it might hurt, if he thought what he had to say *had* to be said. Naturally he made mistakes, but all folk heroes are entitled to their mistakes, and seem to be the more believable and human for them. This spirit of utter independence carries over into his screen work. His

Sam Spade and Philip Marlowe and Rick Blaine are men who refuse to kowtow to anyone or anything. They have their own guidelines by which they rule their lives. True, they may bend a few regulations from time to time, but usually it is done for a noble cause or purpose. Rules sometimes need to be changed and breaking them sometimes triggers that change. Young people are the most likely to effect the changes in society the way Bogart would doubtlessly bring them about on screen. Bogart also appeals to the young on a more one-to-one basis. A Gary Cooper is a heroic figure, but somehow seems beyond the reach of common men. Clark Gable was manly and assertive, but he, too, seemed unapproachable. and Jimmy Stewart was just too all-American for any realistic comradeship. It was only Bogart, down-to-earth, full of foibles yet romantic and commanding of respect, that these young people seemed to have found some kinship to.

As a result of his acceptance by not only the young but the public in general, Bogart was able to contribute his own character to screen history, the anti-hero. Bogart was indeed the prototype that set the stage for men like Jason Robards, Jr., George

C. Scott, George Segal, and Dustin Hoffman to emerge as important screen figures in today's films. One no longer needed to look like a young Robert Taylor in order to be a romantic figure. One could now be short, ugly, swear, treat women badly, break the law, or do anything that seemed normal or humanistic and wind up coming out on top, for a welcome change of pace. And one could even win the girl!

Women of all ages seemed to find Bogart particularly appealing, probably because he always maintained a seeming posture of superiority over them, even though he saw them as his equals. Women respected Bogart onscreen because he was smart enough to see through their wiles, and yet was compassionate enough to still accept them. Few women respect passivity in a man, and if a lover like Bogart could combine a bit of animal savagery and even a tinge of lust with tenderness and feeling, then what more could a woman ask for? Just how strong his character was seemed very evident in the parade of leading ladies he came into contact with. Note, for example, how many of his most memorable screen encounters were with women who appeared to be dominating figures on their own, yet who all succumbed to his magnetism. Mary Astor, Ida Lupino, Lizabeth Scott, and Lauren Bacall were all women who would knuckle under to no man, who could give measure for measure for what they got, yet once they met Bogart they seemed to immediately let him become the master of the situation. Perhaps they were playing with him, feeling that once they had him hooked, they could bend him to suit their own desires, like Hepburn in *The African Queen*. Or perhaps they saw in him that certain ambiguity that makes life all the more interesting, that feeling of not knowing what to expect next that makes each day a new and more exciting experience. Whatever their motivation, these women all acted as a vicarious screen substitute for millions of women in the audience who wished they could change places, even briefly, with them and somehow be taken out of their own conventional lives.

Others who respond actively to Bogart's screen image are those who see him not as an individual but rather as a representative of an era that was once important to them (but may have never existed), as the embodiment of thirties and forties' romanticism. In a real world where people seem out of touch with each other emotionally and spiritually, they find it pleasant indeed to return to the safety of Rick's Café Américaine and meet old cinema friends, to absorb these celluloid images into their own lives. The performers become more than merely casual acquaintances, they become as real as one's own relations, and when Sam Spade or Charlie Allnut fades into black with the end title, a part of what they once were and once believed in, fades with them, only to flicker into life again when the film returns for yet another screening. For them, Bogart is their personal, endlessly satisfying phoenix.

Even though Bogart had a very special appeal to select groups for specific reasons, one can safely say that the actor did possess attributes which *all* groups can appreciate. Above all, he seemed to have an integrity that commanded respect and admiration. True, he could be hard, bitter, and shorn of illusions about life, but in the end he always managed to adhere to a particular code of decency and honor that was exemplary. It is *that* Bogart most of us fondly remember, and if in his Sam Spade or Rick or Harry Morgan we saw some noble qualities we have been successful in adapting into our own lives, we are certainly the better off for it. It was fortunate that we had a Humphrey Bogart to show us the way.

BIBLIOGRAPHY

Baxter, John. *Hollywood in the Thirties.* New York: A. S. Barnes, 1968.

Gehman, Richard. *Bogart.* New York: Gold Medal Books and Fawcett Publications, Inc., 1965.

Goodman, Ezra. *Bogey: The Good Bad Guy.* New York: Lyle Stuart, Inc., 1965.

Halliwell, Leslie. *The Filmgoer's Companion.* 3rd. ed. New York: Hill and Wang, 1970.

Higham, Charles, and Joel Greenberg. *Hollywood in the Forties.* New York: A. S. Barnes, 1968.

McCarty, Clifford. *Bogey: The Films of Humphrey Bogart.* New York: Citadel Press, 1965.

The New York Times Film Reviews, 1913-1968. New York: The New York Times and Arno Press, 1970.

Nolan, William F. *John Huston, King Rebel.* California: Sherbourne Press, Inc., 1965.

Ringgold, Gene. *The Films of Bette Davis.* New York: Citadel Press, 1966.

Sennett, Ted. *Warner Brothers Presents.* New York: Arlington House, 1971.

Warner, Jack, and Dean Jennings. *My First Hundred Years in Hollywood.* New York: Random House, 1965.

THE FILMS OF HUMPHREY BOGART

The director's name follows the release date. A (c)
following the release date indicates that the film was
in color. Sp indicates Screenplay and b/o indicates
based/on.

1. A DEVIL WITH WOMEN. Fox., 1930. *Irving Cummings.*
Sp: Dudley Nichols & Henry M. Johnson. B/o novel *Dust and
Sun* by Clements Ripley. Cast: Victor McLaglen, Mona Maris,
Luana Alcaniz. HB was a rich gadabout who kept getting in the
way of Soldier of Fortune McLaglen as he tracked down a Mex-
ican bandit.

2. UP THE RIVER. Fox., 1930. *John Ford.* Sp: Maurine Wat-
kins. Cast: Spencer Tracy, Claire Luce, Warren Hymer, William
Collier, Sr., Gaylord Pendleton, Morgan Wallace. HB was a
young ex-convict whose happiness with a female ex-convict is
threatened by exposure of their past by a crook. Spencer Tracy's
first film.

3. BODY AND SOUL. Fox., 1931. *Alfred Santell.* Sp: Jules
Furthman. B/o play *Squadrons* by A. E. Thomas. Cast: Charles
Farrell, Elissa Landi, Myrna Loy, Donald Dillaway, Craufurd
Kent. HB was a World War I pilot who got killed attacking a Ger-
man observation balloon.

4. BAD SISTER. Univ., 1931. *Hobart Henley.* Sp: Raymond L.
Schrock & Tom Reed. B/o story *The Flirt* by Booth Tarkington.
Cast: Conrad Nagel, Sidney Fox, Bette Davis, ZaSu Pitts, Slim
Summerville. In his first role as a heavy, HB was a swindler in
this soap-opera about a spoiled daughter of a rich industrialist.
Sidney Fox and Bette Davis made their screen debuts in this
film.

5. WOMEN OF ALL NATIONS. Fox., 1931. *Raoul Walsh.* Sp: Barry Connors. Cast: Victor McLaglen, Edmund Lowe, Greta Nissen, El Brendel, Fifi Dorsay, Bela Lugosi. HB had a very minor role as a Marine in this story concerning the further adventures of Sgt. Flagg and Sgt. Quirt, two characters created by McLaglen and Lowe in *What Price Glory?*

6. A HOLY TERROR. Fox., 1931. *Irving Cummings.* Sp: Ralph Block. B/o novel *Trailin'* by Max Brand. Cast: George O'Brien, Sally Eilers, James Kirkwood, Stanley Fields, Robert Warwick. HB was a jealous ranch foreman and heavy in this routine B-Western.

7. LOVE AFFAIR. Col., 1932. *Thornton Freeland.* Sp: Jo Swerling & Dorothy Howell. B/o story by Ursula Parrott. Cast: Dorothy Mackaill, Jack Kennedy, Bradley Page, Astrid Allwyn. HB was an aviator-engineer in his first leading role in this romantic story of a rich young heiress' love affair.

8. BIG CITY BLUES. WB., 1932. *Mervyn LeRoy.* Sp: Ward Morehouse & Lillie Howard. B/o play *New York Town* by Ward Morehouse. Cast: Joan Blondell, Eric Linden, Evalyn Knapp, Guy Kibbee, Lyle Talbot. HB was billed tenth as a partygoer who is a suspect, among others, in a murder.

9. THREE ON A MATCH. WB., 1932. *Mervyn LeRoy.* Sp: Lucien Hubbard, Kubec Glasmon, & John Bright. B/o story by Kubec Glasmon & John Bright. Cast: Joan Blondell, Warren William, Ann Dvorak, Bette Davis, Lyle Talbot, Glenda Farrell, Frankie Darro. HB was a gangster hired to kidnap a young boy in this tale about the tangled lives of three girl friends.

10. MIDNIGHT. Univ., 1934. *Chester Erskine.* Sp: Chester Erskine. B/o play by Paul & Claire Sifton. Cast: Sidney Fox, O. P. Heggie, Henry Hull, Margaret Wycherly, Richard Whorf. HB was a gangster killed by Fox when he spurned her. This film was done in New York.

11. THE PETRIFIED FOREST. WB., 1936. *Archie Mayo.* Sp: Charles Kenyon & Delmer Daves. B/o play by Robert E. Sherwood. Cast: Leslie Howard, Bette Davis, Genevieve Tobin, Dick

Foran, Joseph Sawyer, Charley Grapewin. HB was Duke Mantee, a merciless gangster holding a group of people captive in a gas station-restaurant. One of his most famous roles.

12. BULLETS OR BALLOTS. WB., 1936. *William Keighley*. Sp: Seton I. Miller. B/o story by Martin Mooney & Seton I. Miller. Cast: Edward G. Robinson, Joan Blondell, Barton MacLane, Frank McHugh. HB was a racketeer-killer and Robinson the cop who finally got him.

13. TWO AGAINST THE WORLD. WB., 1936. *William McGann*. Sp: Michel Jacoby. B/o play *Five Star Final* by Louis Weitzenkorn. Cast: Beverly Roberts, Henry O'Neill, Helen MacKellar. In this remake of *Five Star Final* HB was a station manager who turns against his bosses who are using the airwaves for sensationalism.

14. CHINA CLIPPER. WB., 1936. *Ray Enright*. Sp: Frank Wead. Cast: Pat O'Brien, Beverly Roberts, Ross Alexander, Marie Wilson. HB was one of O'Brien's pilots who makes an historic Clipper flight.

15. ISLE OF FURY. WB., 1936. *Frank McDonald*. Sp: Robert Andrews & William Jacobs. B/o novel *The Narrow Corner* by W. Somerset Maugham. Cast: Margaret Lindsay, Donald Woods, Gordon Hart. HB was a fugitive pursued to a lonely island by Woods, who gives up the chase when convinced Bogart has reformed.

16. BLACK LEGION. WB., 1937. *Archie Mayo*. Sp: Abem Finkel & William Wister Haines. B/o story by Robert Lord. Cast: Dick Foran, Ann Sheridan, Robert Barrat, Erin O'Brien Moore, Joseph Sawyer. HB was a worker who loses a job position and becomes a hooded vigilante for revenge.

17. THE GREAT O'MALLEY. WB., 1937. *William Dieterle*. Sp: Milton Krims & Tom Reed. B/o story *The Making of O'Malley* by Gerald Beaumont. Cast: Pat O'Brien, Ann Sheridan, Donald Crisp, Henry O'Neill. HB was a man sent to jail for a minor offense by overzealous cop O'Brien who escapes and nearly kills the cop.

18. MARKED WOMAN. WB., 1937. *Lloyd Bacon.* Sp: Robert
Rossen & Abem Finkel. Cast: Bette Davis, Lola Lane, Isabel
Jewell, Eduardo Ciannelli, Mayo Methot. HB was a crusading
District Attorney out to get Ciannelli for his treatment of night-
club "hostesses." Bogart married third wife, Methot, during the
filming.

19. KID GALAHAD. WB., 1937. *Michael Curtiz.* Sp: Seton I.
Miller. B/o novel by Francis Wallace. Cast: Edward G. Robinson,
Bette Davis, Wayne Morris, Jane Bryan, Harry Carey, William
Haade, HB was a gangster fight manager double-crossed by
Robinson.

20. SAN QUENTIN. WB., 1937. *Lloyd Bacon.* Sp: Peter Milne &
Humphrey Cobb. B/o story by Robert Tasker & John Bright.
Cast: Pat O'Brien, Ann Sheridan, Barton MacLane, Joseph Saw-
yer, Veda Ann Borg. Familiar prison drama with O'Brien as yard
Captain trying to do good and HB as a prisoner who nearly ruins
things, but who turns out all right at the end.

21. DEAD END. UA., 1937. *William Wyler.* Sp: Lillian Hellman.
B/o play by Sidney Kingsley. Cast: Sylvia Sidney, Joel McCrea,
Wendy Barrie, Claire Trevor, Allen Jenkins, Dead End Kids. HB
was a gangster who returned to his old haunts in one of his best
roles of the Thirties.

22. STAND-IN. UA., 1937. *Tay Garnett.* Sp: Gene Towne & Gra-
ham Baker. B/o story by Clarence Budington Kelland. Cast: Leslie Howard, Joan Blondell, Alan Mowbray, Jack Carson. HB was
a producer-editor who helped efficiency expert Howard save a
Hollywood studio.

23. SWING YOUR LADY. WB., 1938. *Ray Enright.* Sp: Joseph
Schrank & Maurice Leo. B/o play by Kenyon Nicholson &
Charles Robinson. Cast: Frank McHugh, Louise Fazenda, Nat
Pendleton, Penny Singleton, Allen Jenkins. HB was the manager
of wrestler Pendleton in one of the worst roles of Bogart's career.

24. CRIME SCHOOL. WB., 1938. *Lewis Seiler.* Sp: Crane Wilbur & Vincent Sherman. B/o story by Crane Wilbur. Cast: Gale
Page, Dead End Kids, Cy Kendall, Weldon Heyburn. HB was a

Commissioner of Correction who took over the job from a sadistic predecessor.

25. MEN ARE SUCH FOOLS. WB., 1938. *Busby Berkeley.* Sp: Norman Reilly Raine & Horace Jackson. B/o novel by Faith Baldwin. Cast: Wayne Morris, Priscilla Lane, Hugh Herbert, Penny Singleton, Mona Barrie. HB was a radio contact man who became involved in a complicated series of romantic entanglements.

26. THE AMAZING DR. CLITTERHOUSE. WB., 1938. *Anatole Litvak.* Sp: John Wexley & John Huston. B/o play by Barre Lyndon. Cast: Edward G. Robinson, Claire Trevor, Allen Jenkins, Donald Crisp, Gale Page, Ward Bond. HB was a jewel thief called Rocks Valentine who Robinson studied as part of his research on a book dealing with the physiological reactions of criminals.

27. RACKET BUSTERS. WB., 1938. *Lloyd Bacon.* Sp: Robert Rossen & Leonardo Bercovici. Cast: George Brent, Gloria Dickson, Allen Jenkins, Walter Abel, Henry O'Neill, Penny Singleton. HB was the head of a gang who tried to muscle in on Manhattan's trucking business.

28. ANGELS WITH DIRTY FACES. WB., 1938. *Michael Curtiz.* Sp: John Wexley & Warren Duff. B/o story by Rowland Brown. Cast: James Cagney, Pat O'Brien, Ann Sheridan, George Bancroft, Billy Halop, Bobby Jordan, Leo Gorcey, Gabriel Dell, Huntz Hall, Bernard Punsley. HB was a double-crossing ex-lawyer who was prospering as a nightclub owner until Cagney killed him. One of Bogart's most popular films, although he had only a relatively small part.

29. KING OF THE UNDERWORLD. WB., 1939. *Lewis Seiler.* Sp: George Bricker & Vincent Sherman. B/o story *Dr. Socrates* by W. R. Burnett. Cast: Kay Francis, James Stephenson, John Eldredge. HB was a gangster on the run who is ultimately captured when Francis temporarily blinds him.

30. THE OKLAHOMA KID. WB., 1939. *Lloyd Bacon.* Sp: Warren Duff, Robert Buckner & Edward E. Paramore. B/o story by Edward E. Paramore & Wally Klein. Cast: James Cagney, Rosemary Lane, Donald Crisp, Ward Bond. HB was the head of an

outlaw gang responsible for the hanging of Cagney's father.

31. DARK VICTORY. WB., 1939. *Edmund Goulding.* Sp: Casey Robinson. B/o play by George Emerson Brewer, Jr. & Bertram Bloch. Cast: Bette Davis, George Brent, Geraldine Fitzgerald, Ronald Reagan, Henry Travers. HB was terribly miscast as an Irish groom in this favorite Davis tearjerker.

32. YOU CAN'T GET AWAY WITH MURDER. WB., 1939. *Lewis Seiler.* Sp: Robert Buckner, Don Ryan, & Kenneth Gamet. B/o play *Chalked Out* by Warden Lewis E. Lawes & Jonathan Finn. Cast: Billy Halop, Gale Page, John Litel, Henry Travers, Harold Huber, Joseph Sawyer. HB was a tough gangster sent to prison with Halop, whom he tries to kill when he fears the kid will turn informer.

33. THE ROARING TWENTIES. WB., 1939. *Raoul Walsh.* Sp: Jerry Wald, Richard Macaulay, & Robert Rossen. B/o story by Mark Hellinger. Cast: James Cagney, Priscilla Lane, Gladys George, Jeffrey Lynn, Frank McHugh, Paul Kelly, Joseph Sawyer. Stylish melodrama with HB as an ex-war buddy of Cagney and Lynn who becomes a big time racketeer and turns against them when they threaten his position.

34. THE RETURN OF DOCTOR X. WB., 1939. *Vincent Sherman.* Sp: Lee Katz. B/o story *The Doctor's Secret* by William J. Makin. Cast: Wayne Morris, Rosemary Lane, Dennis Morgan, John Litel. In one of his most bizarre portrayals, HB was a vampire preying upon young girls for blood.

35. INVISIBLE STRIPES. WB., 1939. *Lloyd Bacon.* Sp: Warren Duff. B/o story by Jonathan Finn from book by Warden Lewis E. Lawes. Cast: George Raft, Jane Bryan, William Holden, Flora Robson, Paul Kelly, Henry O'Neill, Marc Lawrence, Leo Gorcey. HB was the gangster pal of Raft and both were shot down when they turned against their own gang.

36. VIRGINIA CITY. WB., 1940. *Michael Curtiz.* Sp: Robert Buckner. Cast: Errol Flynn, Miriam Hopkins, Randolph Scott, Frank McHugh, Alan Hale, Guinn "Big Boy" Williams, John Litel. HB was the head of an outlaw band who is hired by Scott to

help the Confederacy get a huge gold shipment.

37. IT ALL CAME TRUE. WB., 1940. *Lewis Seiler.* Sp: Michael Fessier & Lawrence Kimble. B/o story *Better Than Life* by Louis Bromfield. Cast: Ann Sheridan, Jeffrey Lynn, ZaSu Pitts, Una O'Connor, John Litel, Grant Mitchell. HB was a gangster who hides out in a rooming house which he finally turns into a nightclub before being captured. A good comedy-drama for the actor.

38. BROTHER ORCHID. WB., 1940. *Lloyd Bacon.* Sp: Earl Baldwin. B/o story by Richard Connell. Cast: Edward G. Robinson, Ann Sothern, Donald Crisp, Ralph Bellamy, Allen Jenkins, Cecil Kellaway. HB was a gangster out to eliminate Robinson and take over as top man of the rackets.

39. THEY DRIVE BY NIGHT. WB., 1940. *Raoul Walsh.* Sp: Jerry Wald & Richard Macaulay. B/o novel *Long Haul* by A. I. Bezzerides. Cast: George Raft, Ann Sheridan, Ida Lupino, Gale Page, Alan Hale, Roscoe Karns, John Litel, George Tobias. HB was Raft's brother and lost an arm as they battled to acquire their own trucking business.

40. HIGH SIERRA. WB., 1941. *Raoul Walsh.* Sp: John Huston & W. R. Burnett. B/o novel by W. R. Burnett. Cast: Ida Lupino, Alan Curtis, Arthur Kennedy, Joan Leslie, Henry Hull, Henry Travers, Jerome Cowan, Cornel Wilde. HB was escaped killer Roy Earle. This film boosted Bogart to stardom and remains as one of his finest screen roles.

41. THE WAGONS ROLL AT NIGHT. WB., 1941. *Ray Enright.* Sp: Fred Niblo, Jr. & Barry Trivers. B/o novel *Kid Galahad* by Francis Wallace. Cast: Sylvia Sidney, Eddie Albert, Joan Leslie, Sig Rumann. HB was the head of a traveling carnival in this remake of *Kid Galahad* which found Albert playing a lion tamer whereas in the original Wayne Morris had played a boxer. Bogart received top billing for the first time in a major film.

42. THE MALTESE FALCON. WB., 1941. *John Huston.* Sp: John Huston. B/o novel by Dashiell Hammett. Cast: Mary Astor, Gladys George, Peter Lorre, Barton MacLane, Lee Patrick, Sydney Greenstreet, Ward Bond, Jerome Cowan, Elisha Cook, Jr.,

Walter Huston. HB played detective Sam Spade in not only one of his best roles, but perhaps in one of the best pictures of all time. It was also John Huston's first directorial effort.

43. ALL THROUGH THE NIGHT. WB., 1942. *Vincent Sherman.* Sp: Leonard Spigelgass & Edwin Gilbert. B/o story by Leonard Q. Ross (Leo Rosten) & Leonard Spigelgass. Cast: Conrad Veidt, Kaaren Verne, Jane Darwell, Frank McHugh, Peter Lorre, Judith Anderson, William Demarest, Jackie Gleason, Phil Silvers, Wallace Ford, Barton MacLane. HB was a Runyonesque tough guy in search of murderers and spies during World War II.

44. THE BIG SHOT. WB., 1942. *Lewis Seiler.* Sp: Bertram Millhauser, Abem Finkel, & Daniel Fuchs. Cast: Irene Manning, Richard Travis, Susan Peters, Stanley Ridges, Chick Chandler, Howard da Silva. HB was a gangster who was framed and sent to prison but who breaks out and kills the man responsible.

45. ACROSS THE PACIFIC. WB., 1942. *John Huston.* Sp: Richard Macaulay. B/o story *Aloha Means Goodbye* by Robert Carson. Cast: Mary Astor, Sydney Greenstreet, Victor Sen Yung, Charles Halton. HB was an Army Intelligence officer who breaks up an enemy plot to blow up the Panama Canal.

46. CASABLANCA. WB., 1943. *Michael Curtiz.* Sp: Julius J. & Philip G. Epstein and Howard Koch. B/o play *Everybody Comes to Rick's* by Murray Burnett & Joan Alison. Cast: Ingrid Bergman, Paul Henreid, Claude Rains, Conrad Veidt, Sydney Greenstreet, Peter Lorre, S. Z. Sakall, Dooley Wilson. HB was Rick, the owner of a nightclub in Casablanca that became the meeting place for refugees fleeing from Europe to Lisbon. This film turned Bogart into a romantic leading man and is one of the most famous films of the Forties. Bogart received his first Academy Award nomination for his role, and the film won Academy Awards for Best Picture of 1943, Best Screenplay, and Best Director.

47. ACTION IN THE NORTH ATLANTIC. WB., 1943. *Lloyd Bacon.* Sp: John Howard Lawson. B/o novel by Guy Gilpatric. Cast: Raymond Massey, Alan Hale, Julie Bishop, Ruth Gordon, Sam Levene, Dane Clark, Kane Richmond, Chick Chandler,

Peter Whitney. HB was the heroic first mate of a tanker during World War II.

48. THANK YOUR LUCKY STARS. WB., 1943. *David Butler*. Sp: Norman Panama, Melvin Frank, & James V. Kern. B/o story by Everett Freeman & Arthur Schwartz. Cast: Eddie Cantor, Bette Davis, Olivia de Havilland, Errol Flynn, Dinah Shore, Ida Lupino, John Garfield, Joan Leslie, Dennis Morgan, Jack Carson. Alexis Smith. HB did a brief backstage bit as himself.

49. SAHARA. Col., 1943. *Zoltan Korda*. Sp: John Howard Lawson & Zoltan Korda. B/o story by Philip MacDonald based on an incident in the Soviet film *The Thirteen*. Cast: Bruce Bennett, J. Carrol Naish, Lloyd Bridges, Rex Ingram, Dan Duryea. HB was a tank commander who holds off a German battalion with the aid of only a few men at a desert oasis.

50. PASSAGE TO MARSEILLE. WB., 1944. *Michael Curtiz*. Sp: Casey Robinson & Jack Moffitt. B/o novel *Men Without Country* by Charles Nordhoff & James Norman Hall. Cast: Claude Rains, Michele Morgan, Philip Dorn, Sydney Greenstreet, Peter Lorre, George Tobias, John Loder, Helmut Dantine. HB was a French journalist who escaped from Devil's Island, prevented the takeover of a French ship by Fascists and then became a member of a Free French bomber squadron.

51. TO HAVE AND HAVE NOT. WB., 1945. *Howard Hawks*. Sp: Jules Furthman & William Faulkner. B/o novel by Ernest Hemingway. Cast: Walter Brennan, Lauren Bacall, Dolores Moran, Hoagy Carmichael, Sheldon Leonard. HB was the owner of a small fishing boat who becomes involved in smuggling a French underground leader and his wife out of Martinique. Bacall's first film.

52. CONFLICT. WB., 1945. *Curtis Bernhardt*. Sp: Arthur T. Horman & Dwight Taylor. B/o story by Robert Siodmak & Alfred Neumann. Cast: Alexis Smith, Sydney Greenstreet, Rose Hobart. HB played a man who murdered his wife and is finally trapped into showing his guilt by Greenstreet.

53. THE BIG SLEEP. WB., 1946. *Howard Hawks*. Sp: William

Faulkner, Leigh Brackett, & Jules Furthman. B/o novel by Raymond Chandler. Cast: Lauren Bacall, John Ridgely, Martha Vickers, Dorothy Malone, Regis Toomey, Bob Steele, Elisha Cook, Jr. HB was private detective Philip Marlowe on the trail of blackmailers and killers. A confusing film but a popular one with Bogart fans.

54. DEAD RECKONING. Col., 1947. *John Cromwell.* Sp: Oliver H. P. Garrett & Steve Fisher. B/o story by Gerald Adams & Sidney Biddell. Cast: Lizabeth Scott, Morris Carnovsky, Marvin Miller, Wallace Ford, Ruby Dandridge. HB was a paratrooper who sought out the murderer of a pal.

55. THE TWO MRS. CARROLLS. WB., 1947. *Peter Godfrey.* Sp: Thomas Job. B/o play by Martin Vale. Cast: Barbara Stanwyck, Alexis Smith, Nigel Bruce. HB was a homicidal artist who killed his first wife and was working on a second. Very likely Bogart's worst film.

56. DARK PASSAGE. WB., 1947. *Delmer Daves.* Sp: Delmer Daves. B/o novel by David Goodis. Cast: Lauren Bacall, Bruce Bennett, Agnes Moorehead, Tom D'Andrea. HB was an innocent man framed for the murder of his wife who escapes from prison and tracks down the real killer. Interesting in its use of a subjective camera during early sequences.

57. THE TREASURE OF THE SIERRA MADRE. WB., 1948. *John Huston.* Sp: John Huston. B/o novel by B. Traven. Cast: Walter Huston, Tim Holt, Bruce Bennett, Barton MacLane, Alfonso Bedoya, Bobby Blake, John Huston, Jack Holt. HB gave one of his most memorable performances as Fred C. Dobbs, an out-of-work American who sets out with two partners to search for gold. The film won two Academy Awards for John Huston's direction and writing and a third went to Walter Huston as Best Supporting Actor. A screen classic.

58. KEY LARGO. WB., 1948. *John Huston.* Sp: Richard Brooks & John Huston. B/o play by Maxwell Anderson. Cast: Edward G. Robinson, Lauren Bacall, Lionel Barrymore, Claire Trevor, Thomas Gomez, Marc Lawrence. HB was a war veteran who found himself in an isolated hotel taken over by Robinson and his gang.

Claire Trevor won an Academy Award for her role as Gaye Dawn.

59. KNOCK ON ANY DOOR. Col., 1949. *Nicholas Ray.* Sp: Daniel Taradash & John Monks, Jr. B/o novel by Willard Motley. Cast: John Derek, George Macready, Allene Roberts, Susan Perry, Mickey Knox. HB was an attorney defending a young hoodlum in a murder trial. This was Bogart's first film produced under his Santana Productions.

60. TOKYO JOE. Col., 1949. *Stuart Heisler.* Sp: Cyril Hume & Bertram Millhauser. B/o story by Steve Fisher. Cast: Alexander Knox, Florence Marly, Sessue Hayakawa, Jerome Courtland, Gordon Jones. HB was an ex-Army pilot who returned to Japan and found himself involved with an ex-wife and a plot to smuggle Japanese war criminals back into Japan.

61. CHAIN LIGHTNING. WB., 1950. *Stuart Heisler.* Sp: Liam O'Brien & Vincent Evans. B/o story by J. Redmond Prior. Cast: Eleanor Parker, Raymond Massey, Richard Whorf, James Brown, Roy Roberts. HB was a test pilot trying out new jet planes and an ejection cockpit.

62. IN A LONELY PLACE. Col., 1950. *Nicholas Ray.* Sp: Andrew Solt. B/o novel by Dorothy B. Hughes. Cast: Gloria Grahame, Frank Lovejoy, Carl Benton Reid, Art Smith, Jeff Donnell, Martha Stewart. HB was a Hollywood writer suspected of murder and given to violent psychotic rages. The best of his four Santana productions released through Columbia.

63. THE ENFORCER. WB., 1951. *Bretaigne Windust.* Sp: Martin Rackin. Cast: Zero Mostel, Ted De Corsia, Everett Sloane, Roy Roberts, Bob Steele, King Donovan. HB was an Assistant District Attorney out to get the head of Murder, Inc. This was Bogart's final film for Warner Brothers.

64. SIROCCO. Col., 1951. *Curtis Bernhardt.* Sp: A. I. Bezzerides & Hans Jacoby. B/o novel *Coup de Grace* by Joseph Kessel. Cast: Marta Toren, Lee J. Cobb, Everett Sloane, Gerald Mohr, Zero Mostel, Onslow Stevens, Ludwig Donath, Harry Guardino. HB was a gunrunner who divided his loyalties between the French and the Syrians in 1925.

65. THE AFRICAN QUEEN. UA., 1951. (c) *John Huston.* Sp: James Agee & John Huston. B/o novel by C. S. Forester. Cast: Katharine Hepburn, Robert Morley, Peter Bull, Theodore Bikel. HB was the skipper of an old river launch who is persuaded by Hepburn to attack a German gunboat. This is one of Bogart's greatest roles and won him an Academy Award as Best Actor of 1951.

66. DEADLINE—U.S.A. 20th Cen.-Fox., 1952. *Richard Brooks.* Sp: Richard Brooks. Cast: Ethel Barrymore, Kim Hunter, Ed Begley, Warren Stevens, Paul Stewart, Martin Gabel, Joe De Santis. HB was a crusading managing editor out to save his paper and break up a crime syndicate.

67. BATTLE CIRCUS. MGM., 1953. *Richard Brooks.* Sp: Richard Brooks. B/o story by Allen Rivkin & Laura Kerr. Cast: June Allyson, Keenan Wynn, Robert Keith, William Campbell, Steve Forrest. HB was a Major in charge of a field hospital during the Korean War.

68. BEAT THE DEVIL. UA., 1954. *John Huston.* Sp: John Huston & Truman Capote. Cast: Jennifer Jones, Gina Lollobrigida, Robert Morley, Peter Lorre, Edward Underdown. HB was a stranded adventurer who teams up with an outlandish group of conspirators to obtain an African uranium mine. Bogart's final film with John Huston, and one on which he was co-producer.

69. THE CAINE MUTINY. Col., 1954. (c) *Edward Dmytryk.* Sp: Stanley Roberts. B/o novel by Herman Wouk. Cast: Jose Ferrer, Van Johnson, Fred MacMurray, Robert Francis, May Wynn, Tom Tully, E. G. Marshall, Arthur Franz, Lee Marvin, Warner Anderson. HB gave one of his most powerful portrayals as Captain Queeg. Bogart received his third Academy Award nomination for this role.

70. SABRINA. Par., 1954. *Billy Wilder.* Sp: Billy Wilder, Samuel Taylor, & Ernest Lehman. B/o play *Sabrina Fair* by Samuel Taylor. Cast: Audrey Hepburn, William Holden, Walter Hampden, John Williams, Martha Hyer. HB was a rich, stuffy businessman who fell in love with a chauffeur's daughter.

71. **THE BAREFOOT CONTESSA.** UA., 1954. (c) *Joseph L. Mankiewicz.* Sp: Joseph L. Mankiewicz. Cast: Ava Gardner, Edmond O'Brien, Marius Goring, Valentina Cortesa, Rossano Brazzi, Elizabeth Sellars, Warren Stevens, Bessie Love. HB was a washed-up movie director who regained his stature when he discovered Gardner dancing in a Madrid cafe and starred her in a new movie. O'Brien won an Academy Award for his role in the film.

72. **WE'RE NO ANGELS.** Par., 1955. (c) *Michael Curtiz.* Sp: Ranald MacDougall. B/o play *La Cuisine des Anges* by Albert Husson. Cast: Aldo Ray, Peter Ustinov, Joan Bennett, Basil Rathbone, Leo G. Carroll. HB was an escaped prisoner from Devil's Island who, with his two friends, saves a family from losing their store in a comedy-drama that was a misfire.

73. **THE LEFT HAND OF GOD.** 20th Cen.-Fox., 1955. (c) *Edward Dmytryk.* Sp: Alfred Hayes. B/o novel by William E. Barrett. Cast: Gene Tierney, Lee J. Cobb, Agnes Moorehead, E. G. Marshall, Victor Sen Yung. HB was an American flyer who was forced down in China during World War II and joined up with a War Lord, whom he eventually tried to escape from by donning priest's robes.

74. **THE DESPERATE HOURS.** Par., 1955. *William Wyler.* Sp: Joseph Hayes. B/o novel and play by Joseph Hayes. Cast: Fredric March, Arthur Kennedy, Martha Scott, Dewey Martin, Gig Young, Mary Murphy, Richard Eyer, Robert Middleton. HB was a vicious escaped convict who, with two accomplices, takes over the home of a respectable family and terrorizes them. Bogart's first tough gangster role since *High Sierra.*

75. **THE HARDER THEY FALL.** Col., 1956. *Mark Robson.* Sp: Philip Yordan. B/o novel by Budd Schulberg. Cast: Rod Steiger, Jan Sterling, Mike Lane, Max Baer, Jersey Joe Walcott, Edward Andrews, Harold J. Stone, Carlos Montalban, Nehemiah Persoff. In his final screen appearance HB played an ex-sports writer who got involved in helping a crooked fight promoter push a fighter to the top through a series of fixed fights. A first-rate ending to Bogart's career.

Humphrey Bogart also made brief unbilled screen appearances in the following films.

1. BROADWAY'S LIKE THAT. WB., 1930. HB had a very minor role in this one-reel musical which starred Ruth Etting and Joan Blondell.

2. REPORT FROM THE FRONT. 1944. In this three-minute trailer prepared by the Red Cross, HB and his wife Mayo Methot were shown during their overseas war tours. He narrated and asked for donations from the audience.

3. HOLLYWOOD VICTORY CARAVAN. Par., 1945. In this two-reel short HB was one of a large contingent of stars aboard a train headed for a Washington rally. He made an appeal for people to buy Victory Loan Bonds.

4. TWO GUYS FROM MILWAUKEE. WB., 1946. HB made a brief gag appearance with Bacall in an airplane sequence in this Dennis Morgan-Jack Carson comedy.

5. ALWAYS TOGETHER. WB., 1948. HB had a brief bit doing a take-off on *Stella Dallas* as he played an outcast father weeping against a rainy windowpane.

6. U. S. SAVINGS BOND TRAILER. MGM., 1952. HB was again asking people to buy bonds in this brief clip attached to MGM newsreels for July 25-26.

7. ROAD TO BALI. Par., 1952. A clip of Bogart from *The African Queen* was used as a gag in this Hope-Crosby comedy.

8. THE LOVE LOTTERY. Rank., 1953. As a favor to David Niven, HB did a small walk-on in this British comedy.

Humphrey Bogart also appeared in caricatures in numerous WB cartoons (like 8-BALL BUNNY in which he keeps popping up dressed in his *The Treasure of the Sierra Madre* outfit and asking Bugs Bunny if he can spare some money to "help a poor American who's down on his luck," a line from the film.)

INDEX

(Page numbers italicized indicate photographs)

157

ABOUT THE AUTHOR

Alan G. Barbour is the author of *Days of Thrills and Adventure, A Thousand and One Delights,* and *The Thrill of it All,* all reflecting his lifelong devotion to films. He is also the editor and publisher of *Screen Facts* magazine. He lives in Kew Gardens, New York.

ABOUT THE EDITOR

Ted Sennett has been attending and enjoying movies since the age of two. He has written about films for magazines and newspapers, and is the author of *Warner Brothers Presents,* a survey of the great Warners films of the thirties and forties. A publishing executive, he lives in New Jersey with his wife and three children.